First published in Great Britain in 2014 by Unkant Publishers, London

Introduction and Preface copyright © David Black 2014
The rights of the author of this work have been asserted in accordance with the Copyright, Designs and Patents Act 1998.

Designed by Keith Fisher and Andy Wilson
Cover illustration by Andy Wilson

British Library Cataloguing-in-Publication Data
A CIP catalogue record for this book is available from the British Library
A Paperback Original

ISBN 978-0-9926509-1-9
1 3 5 7 9 10 8 6 4 2

All rights reserved. No part of this publication may be reproduced, stored in a retrieval system, or transmitted in any form or by any means without the prior permission of the publisher, nor be otherwise circulated in a binding or cover other than that in which it is published and without a similar condition being imposed on the subsequent purchaser.

Set in Unkant Jensen
www.unkant.com

Helen Macfarlane
Red Republican

The complete annotated writings, including the first translation of the Communist Manifesto

Edited and Introduced by
David Black

Unkant Publishers
London
2014

Contents

Foreward	i
Helen Macfarlane: A Biographical-Philosophical Introduction	v
The Scottish governess who translated the Communist Manifesto	v
Helen Macfarlane's pantheist-Hegelian-Marxism	xi
Why a 'hobgoblin'?	xxii
Helen Macfarlane's break with George Julian Harney	xxvi
After Chartism—travels and tragedy	xxix

Democratic Review
April 1850 to September 1850

Remarks on the Times–Apropos of Certain Passages in No.1 of Thomas Carlyle's Latter-day Pamphlets	1
Intrigues of the Middle Class 'Reformers'	23
A Bird's Eye View of the Glorious British Constitution	29

Red Republican
June 1850 to November 1850

Chartism in 1850...	37
The Red Flag in 1850	47
Fine Words (Household or Otherwise) Butter No Parsnips	53
Middle-class Dodges and Proletarian Gullibility in 1850	59
Democratic Organization	65
Proceedings of the Peace-at-any-Price Middle-Class-Humbugs	71
The 'Morning Post' and the Woman Flogger	79
The Democratic and Social Republic	83
Labour *versus* Capital: Two Chapters on Humbug	91

Friend of the People
21 & 26 December 1850

Signs of the Times. Red-Stockings *versus* Lawn-Sleeves	103

Red Republican
November 1850

Introduction by George Julian Harney	117
Manifesto of the German Communist Party	119
Chapter one: bourgeois and proletarians	120
Chapter two: proletarians and communists	131
Chapter three: socialist and communist literature	139
Position of the communists in relation to the various existing opposition parties	148
Index	151

David Black

David Black (born 1950) was brought up in Newcastle-upon-Tyne. After leaving Middlesex Polytechnic he worked for Roland and Claire Muldoon's Cartoon Archetypical Slogan Theatre (C.A.S.T.) and later for New Variety. In the 1980s he got into freelance journalism. In 1999 he co-founded *The Hobgoblin—a Journal of Marxist-Humanism*.

His previous books are *Acid: A New Secret History of LSD*, *Helen Macfarlane: A Feminist, Revolutionary Journalist and Philosopher in Mid-Nineteenth Century England*, *1839: The Chartist Insurrection*, (co-authored with Chris Ford), and *The Philosophical Roots of Anti-Capitalism: Essays on History, Culture and Dialectical Thought*.

The editors and publishers would like to thank Keith Fisher of the Association of Musical Marxists for his hard work typing out Macfarlane's essays from photocopies of Chartist newspapers: they were set in such narrow columns no optical scanner on earth was able to scan them.

Foreword

Talking of the destructive nature of egoistic desire—its satisfaction that the other is nothing—Hegel made room for further development, an empirical moment which might surprise those who think German Idealism only ever allowed for abstraction: *"In this satisfaction, however, experience makes it* [the simple 'I'] *aware that the object has its own independence"*.[1] History is such an independent object, and provided it is researched by genuine desire, it can jolt self-satisfaction out of its destructive circuits. Since Samuel Taylor Coleridge's fumbling initiation, German philosophy has provided the Anglophone world with ample opportunity for both desirous egoisim and destructive self-satisfaction, but historical research has recently unearthed an independent object to reshape our ideas, not just of the reception of Hegel in English, but of what we actually think about *Everything*.

This 'independent object' is the Chartist journalism of Helen Macfarlane in 1850, admired by Karl Marx as the work of a *'rara avis'* with truly 'original ideas,' but forgotten by everyone since, including all the official 'Marxists.'

In *Radical Philosophy* #186, David Charlston used graphs of statistical density to demonstrate how the 'objective' treatment of Hegel by translators like Terry Pinkard has served to *"secularize and depoliticise Hegel"*. We found Charlston's coupling an encouragement, since it implies a radical break with today's consensus that rational politics can only start once religious passions

---

1. Hegel, *Phenomenology of Spirit*, tr. A.V. Miller, §175.

have been replaced by secular logic. Macfarlane was addressing working-class radicals whose thinking was made possible by religious categories; her 'Hegelianism' meant that she had no time for the Benthamite programme of 'First Rationalism, then Improvement'; she interpreted Hegel as an application of the revolutionary humanism preached by Jesus and then betrayed by the established Church. This may be why, outflanking 'radical poets' like Shelley and Byron, Macfarlane's polemics have the orotund, unanswerable ring of Shakespeare, Milton and Blake. These texts were written to be read aloud, in taverns where illiterate politicos would seize a newspaper and cry, 'Who's here can read? I want to know what Feargus O'Connor is saying about Julian Harney, has the man gone mad?' The Macfarlane revival—she was not only the first translator of the *Manifesto of the Communist Party* (38 years before Samuel Moore's standard one), but the first translator of Hegel's philosophical writings into English—is not simply an independent object to dent the armour of know-it-all Hegelians, it also breaks into the realm of English Literature and its pecking orders;

> ... *the golden age, sung by the poets and prophets of all times and nations, from Hesiod and Isaiah, to Cervantes and Shelley; the Paradise... was never lost, for it lives... this spirit, I say, has descended now upon the multitudes, and has consecrated them to the service of the new—and yet old—religion of Socialist Democracy.*[1]

George Eliot, another nineteenth-century woman (Marian Evans) who also adopted a male soubriquet in print (Macfarlane's was 'Howard Morton'), is revered as a novelist, but if you explore Eliot's critical relationship to Christianity (translator of David Strauss's scandalous *The Life of Jesus, Critically Examined*) parallels with Macfarlane foam forth. Macfarlane's commitment to the Chartist cause has a clarity, a conviction and historical grasp which can make a bid for George Eliot's place at the moral centre of Victorian letters. As the novel form is laid waste by the Booker Prize contingent, reduced to a tawdry opportunity for middle-class confession, moralism and limp satire, Helen Macfarlane's example steps forward; she was already there.

---

1. Macfarlane, 'Chartism in 1850', Red Republican, June 22 1850. See p. 37 below.

So much for the why-and-who. But *philosophy?* Macfarlane's Hegel has none of the anxious complexitudes of Alexandre Kojève's famous lectures—unfortunate template for the French (and now Anglophone) reception of Hegel—which resemble nothing so much as someone tensely and lengthily diffusing a bomb ('𝔇𝔦𝔞𝔩𝔢𝔨𝔱𝔦𝔨' sprayed on the side). For Macfarlane, Hegel is quite simply a translation of Jesus's revolutionary, egalitarian humanism into a world without gods or mystery.

Following the publication of this, her three-part essay in the *Democratic Review*, Macfarlane adopted the nom de plume 'Howard Morton'. She did so when she also began to write for Harney's weekly, the *Red Republican*. One obvious reason for Macfarlane 'keeping her head down' behind a male pseudonym must have been the daunting prejudice that would face *any* woman who openly expressed radical political opinions. When two generations earlier, in 1792, Mary Wollstonecraft had published *A Vindication of the Rights of Woman* and set off to Paris to support the French Revolution, she had been attacked by Horace Walpole as a *"hyena in petticoats"*. But even in 1850, British society, in Helen Macfarlane's judgment, condemned itself in *"the position of women, who are regarded by law not as persons but as things, and placed in the same category as children and the insane"*. Just as the storming of the Bastille in 1789 had introduced the *sans culotte* into the demonology of English opinion, so the June Days of 1848 in Paris provided the equally terrifying figure of the 'Red Cap' Republican, now armed not only with the rifle and the pike but also with the damnable doctrines of socialism and communism. In early Victorian England, a female 'Red Republican' who openly proved that she could wield the pen as a revolutionary weapon better than most men, would have been scourged as a danger to public order and decency.

Whilst Harney's *Democratic Review of British Politics, History and Literature* (to give it its full title) was pitched at an 'educated' readership, his new weekly, the *Red Republican* (the name was changed to the Marat-inspired *Friend of the People* in late-1850) was strictly a paper written for, and by, the working class supporters of the Chartists. But to all intents and purposes there is little difference in style and content between what Macfarlane wrote for the *Review* and what she wrote for the *Red Republican*; except that, although she hid her gender, she was entirely open about her 'intellectual' status. In opposing the 'designs' of bourgeois reformers' who failed to recognise that *"property is a Social, not an Individual, Right"*, and identifying the common ground *"on which it appears that all real reformers can meet"* as *"the emancipation of the Wages-Slaves [and] the abolition of the proletariat"*, she adds, with startling humility:

> *Perhaps, my proletarian brothers, you will think I have spoken dogmatically upon this topic. It is earnestness in the good cause, and no desire of thrusting my private opinions upon others, that has induced me to write as above. I know that the opinions, on practical subjects of one whose training has chiefly been among books and literature, are of little value compared with the opinions of men amongst you, whose education has been continuous battle with the stern realities of life. If, therefore, my judgment of these things be mistaken, let my heartfelt devotion to your cause, plead with you on my behalf.*[1]

Macfarlane harnessed the energies of poetry, religion and philosophy to the Chartist cause, energies without which political radicalism, however intellectually stringent—or academically endorsed—is doomed to fail.

Association of Musical Marxists, 30-vii-2014

---

1. Macfarlane, 'Democratic Organisation', *Red Republican*, August 17 1850. See p. 70 below.

Helen Macfarlane: A Biographical-Philosophical Introduction

The Scottish governess who translated the Communist Manifesto

In assessing the character of Rosa Luxemburg, Raya Dunayevskaya—one female revolutionary writing about another—quotes Herman Melville's insight that original characters in fiction are as rare as *"a law-giver, a revolutionizing philosopher, or the founder of a new religion"* in real life. Dunayevskaya quotes Melville to support her own assessment of Luxemburg as one such original in 'real history', one who like Sophocles' Antigone *"combines yesterday, today and tomorrow in such a manner that the new age suddenly experiences a 'shock of recognition', whether that relates to a new lifestyle or the great need for a revolution here and now"*.[1]

To claim that Helen Macfarlane was just such an original character may seem outlandish. As she entered the world of radical journalism in April 1850, only to abruptly leave it in December of that same year, she may be regarded as an interesting footnote to the history of Chartism and Marxism, but a footnote nonetheless. However, when I first came across her essays and articles of 1850—thirteen of them, which no historian had ever bothered to evaluate—her words jumped off the page at me; it struck me that

---

1. Raya Dunayevskaya, *Rosa Luxemburg, Women's Liberation and Marx's Philosophy of Revolution*.

no one had ever before written like this in the English language. In short, Macfarlane was the shooting star of late-Chartist journalism.

In *Helen Macfarlane: A Feminist, Revolutionary Journalist and Philosopher in Mid-19th Century England*[1] I analysed her writings in the context of Marx and Engels' engagement with the English Chartist movement in the 1840s and '50s. I had been able to find very little biographical information and was completely mystified by her fateful 'disappearance' in 1851 from the records of Chartist history. Since 2004 however, new electronic research tools and digitised archives have provided opportunities for unravelling some of the mysteries about Macfarlane's life. Having 'reopened the case' on Macfarlane's biography, I was, in Spring 2012, contacted by Louise Yeoman, a researcher, producer and broadcaster for BBC Radio Scotland, who had read my book and was on the same trail, with a view to producing a 30-minute radio documentary about Helen Macfarlane for her BBC Radio Scotland series *Women With a Past*. I was delighted to participate in her project and share discoveries with such a super-diligent historical researcher. The episode, 'Helen Macfarlane', broadcast on 26 November 2012, was presented by Susan Morrison, and featured interviews with Liz Arthur, Richard Holloway, Louise Yeoman and myself, with Helen Macfarlane's words read by the Scottish actress, Gerda Stevenson.

So, who was Helen Macfarlane? Pending a forthcoming full-length biography—a work-in-progress—I present below the basic facts of her life. As Louise Yeoman writes:

> *It is a truth universally acknowledged, that a period drama must be in want of a feisty heroine who finds love at last. But our heroine, Helen Macfarlane was no fictional character and her life would have shocked Jane Austen's smocks off.*[2]

Helen Macfarlane was born in Barrhead, near Glasgow, on 25 September 1818. The youngest of 11 children, Helen was raised in a family of urbanised gentry descended from a branch of the

---

1. David Black, *Helen Macfarlane: A Feminist, Revolutionary Journalist and Philosopher in Mid-19th Century England*, 2004, Lanham: Lexington Books.

2. Louise Yeoman, 'Helen Macfarlane—the radical feminist admired by Karl Marx,' BBC News, 25 November 2012, *http://www.bbc.co.uk/news/uk-scotland-20475989*.

Gaelic Macfarlane clan, whose domain had been the Barony of Arrochar, near the head of Loch Long in Argyll and Bute. According to the clan genealogy, the line of Helen's family includes several illustrious chiefs who fell fighting the English on such battlefields as Bannockburn and Flodden.

Helen's father, George Macfarlane (1760–1842), owned calico-printing works at Barrhead and at Campsie in the Vale of Leven. Her mother, née Helen Stenhouse (b. 1772), came from another wealthy family of calico-printers. Both families prospered in the production of 'Turkey Red' bandanas, which were very popular fashion items.

A short extract from the BBC Scotland *Women With a Past* documentary:

[Field recording on the site of the Barrhead calico works]

Liz Arthur: There would have been about three hundred people working in the mill. And they would comprise journeymen, the skilled craftsmen who would make the blocks. There would be the apprentices, there would be labourers who did all the dirty work.

Louise Yeoman: And the workforce in these mills, they're highly unionised and one of the things they don't like is when people bring in unskilled labour. Now Helen's family didn't just have the mills here. They branched out in the 1830s and had more Turkey Red dyeing mills in Campsie and in Campsie there was a huge strike when they tried to bring in unskilled labour and the family actually broke the strike by calling in the army. They and the other mill-owning families brought in the Dragoons.

Susan Morrison: Phew, you didn't mess with Dragoons.

Louise Yeoman: And the Macfarlanes are not that radical. They're not revolutionaries. Now the Stenhouses, Helen's mother's people, they might have been a bit more radical. Chartism was the big movement to get votes for working people. Here they were all solid Chartists, solid radicals, so radical even the tulips are radical, because the works manager, his pride and joy were his tulips. They were all beautiful, they all had names, all had pedigrees and his best, his beautiful, tallest, most symmetrical tulips were all named after his favourite radical politicians. So if you're having a works manager who's a convinced radical, maybe the Stenhouses who own the place are a bit radical. Which makes me wonder if Helen drank in her radical politics from her mother's milk.

Susan Morrison: I think it's interesting because it's anti-Jane Austen. It's not someone living at a distance from where their money is made. She looks out the window and she sees exactly where the family's money is coming from.

Liz Arthur: Yes, I think if she was an intelligent girl as she obviously was, she must have been affected and must have been involved in the lives of the people.

Susan Morrison: Red Clydeside in fashion and politics.

Louise Yeoman: Absolutely, all rolled into one. But in a way I feel that it's this background and this history that gives the west of Scotland their vitality and the character that it has today. I think it's continued, that closeness between working people, industry and the middle classes.

Gerda Stevenson [in the studio, reading Helen Macfarlane's translation of the *Communist Manifesto*]: *"In the earlier revolutions a part of the noblesse joined the bourgeoisie, in the present one, a part of the bourgeoisie is joining the Proletariat, and particularly a part of the Bourgeois-ideologists, or middle-class thinkers, who have attained a theoretical knowledge of the whole historical movement".*[1]

In 1842 the Macfarlane mills went under, engulfed by the rising tide of technology-driven competition between Scottish mill owners. The Macfarlanes were utterly ruined. Helen and her sisters and brothers had to sign away everything, including their mills and their fine house at 5 Royal Crescent, Glasgow. In Helen's case, the prospect of a genteel marriage, perhaps to a rising young lawyer or the son of a good merchant, was gone and she had to take employment as a governess. But by this time, Helen's youngest brother, William Stenhouse Macfarlane—the other known radical in the family—was studying organic chemistry in Giessen, Germany under Justus Liebig. Significantly, one of Liebig's greatest admirers was Karl Marx, who studied his works in the 1840s and referred to his findings in *Capital* on how,

---

1. BBC Radio Scotland documentary; series 'Women With a Past', episode 2 'Helen Macfarlane,' broadcast 26 November 2012.

in Liebig's words, *"Great Britain robs all countries of the conditions of their fertility"*—British misrule and ruin of Ireland's rural economy being the prime example. For Liebig, a system of production that took more from nature than it put back could be referred to as a *"robbery system"*, a term that he used to describe industrialised capitalist agriculture.[1] Helen, like her brother William, learned the German language. This allowed her to earn her living as a governess. The year 1848 found her in Vienna when the Revolution against the Habsburg Monarchy broke out, weeks after the overthrow of King Louis Philippe in France. Later, in a critique of Thomas Carlyle, she wrote:

> *I am free to confess that, for me the most joyful of all spectacles possible in these times is the one which Mr Carlyle laments; one which I enjoyed extremely at Vienna, in March 1848, i.e. 'an universal tumbling of impostors...' For it amounts to this, that men are determined to live no longer in lies... Ca ira! And how do men come to perceive that the old social forms are worn out and useless? By the advent of a new Idea...*[2]

In England in 1848, inspired by the revolutionary events in Europe, the Chartist movement once again took to the streets. In April 1848, the Chartists assembled en masse at London's Kennington Common, with the intention of marching on Parliament to present the third Chartist petition for universal male suffrage—and once more to have it voted down by the House of Commons. The Kennington Common mobilisation, which has been mythologised by Labour Historians as 'historic', was met by a huge government deployment of special constables, and dispersed by a rainstorm. Thirty years after the event, Chartist leader George Julian Harney recalled that, compared with the great days of the Chartist Convention of 1839, when the masses were energized and insurrection was 'in the air', the English 1848 was a 'fiasco'.[3]

---

1. John Bellamy Foster, 'Capitalism and the Accumulation of Catastrophe', *Monthly Review*, Vol. 63, Issue 7, December 2011.
2. Helen Macfarlane, 'Democracy—Remarks on the Times apropos of certain passages in no. 1 of Thomas Carlyle's Latter-Day pamphlet' *Democratic Review*, April, May and June 1850.
3. George Julian Harney, 'The Tremendous Uprising, in Three parts', *Newcastle Weekly Chronicle*, 27 December 1888 to 30 January 1889.

Following the defeat of 1848, Feargus O'Connor, Chartist leader and Member of Parliament for Nottingham, argued that the immediate demands of movement (embodied in the six-point 'People's Charter') needed to be 'moderated' in order to win support amongst the radical liberals of the 'Manchester School'. In contrast, Chartist radicals such as Harney called for rebuilding the movement with a socialist and internationalist perspective. To this end Harney, in June 1849, launched a new monthly, the *Democratic Review of British Politics, History and Literature*; and in spring 1850, he resigned his editorship of O'Connor's weekly paper, the *Northern Star*, to set up a new rival weekly, the *Red Republican*.

Following the post-1848 counter-revolutions, Macfarlane returned from Austria to Britain; first residing in Burnley, Lancashire, then in London (her residence is still standing in Great Titchfield Street, in the area now known as Fitzrovia). She began to write for Harney's presses, and associated herself with Karl Marx and Friedrich Engels who, in exile, had taken up residence in London and Manchester respectively (though it is likely that Macfarlane had known them for some time; Marx is known to have visited Vienna during the 1848 Revolution). Macfarlane's first contributions to Harney's *Democratic Review* appeared under her own name in the April, May and June 1850 issues. Then, when she began to write for the *Red Republican* in June 1850, she began using the male nom de plume, 'Howard Morton' (the real identity of 'Morton' was first revealed by A.R. Schoyen in 1958 in his biography of Harney). Her translation of the *Communist Manifesto*—which Harney greeted as *"the most revolutionary document ever given to the world"*—appeared in the *Red Republican* in four parts in November 1850.

Helen Macfarlane's own writings are in part faction-fighting (taking on those in the Chartist movement and trade unions who would compromise with the political representatives of bourgeois 'humbug', 'cant' and 'twaddle'), part social criticism (laying bare the daily deprivations suffered by the 'labouring classes'), and part philosophical reflection on the course of history, from Antiquity to modern times. She takes on the great literary figures of her day, such as Thomas Carlyle, Charles Dickens and Alphonse de Lamartine; and her writings are full of literary references (to Homer, Sophocles, Cervantes, Milton, and Heinrich Heine, etc., etc.) Macfarlane's writings show not only a thorough

Julian Harney

grasp of what would later become known as Marxism, but also a familiarity with what later Marxists, such as Louis Althusser, tried to *"drive back into the night"*, namely the Hegelian dialectic. Historians of philosophy have ignored her role as the first British commentator on, and translator of, the philosophical writings of George Wilhelm Friedrich Hegel (1770–1831).

Helen Macfarlane's pantheist-Hegelian-Marxism

I believe in Spinoza's God who reveals Himself in the orderly harmony of what exists, not in a God who concerns himself with fates and actions of human beings.
Albert Einstein[1]

---

1. P.A. Schipp. Ed. *Albert Einstein: Philosopher Scientist*, Lasalle: Open Court, 1949.

'Pantheism' is usually associated with the belief, attributed to 'Eastern mysticism', that God is identical with all natural things. Pantheism is thus seen as quite alien to the 'canon' of Marxist 'materialism'. For Helen Macfarlane however, pantheism is defined in humanistic terms. It is:

> *the sublime and cheering doctrine of man's infinity—as the oak lies folded up in the acorn... the divine nature (or at least in a manifestation of it which is found only in man) is common to us all... we are bound to do to others, as we would they should do to us. This rule is universally valid, without distinction of birth, age, rank, sex, country, colour, cultivation, or the like.*[1]

These lines represent Macfarlane's reinterpretation of passages by Hegel which she translates. In these Hegel says that in Christianity,

> *we find the doctrine that the whole human race is equal in the sight of God... These modes of representation make freedom independent of rank, birth, cultivation and the like; and the progress which has been made by this means is immense. Yet this mode of viewing the matter is somewhat different from the fact that freedom is an indispensable element in the conception—man. The undefined feeling of this fact has worked for centuries in the dark; the instinct for freedom had produced the most terrible revolutions, but the idea of the innate freedom of man—this knowledge of his own nature—is not old.*[2]

In German philosophy, pantheism first became a 'hot' issue in the 1790s, when young German philosophers such as Hegel, fired up by the Enlightenment and the French Revolution, rejected the idea of a deity who intervenes from outside in human affairs and the universe generally. In this they were influenced by two important, though quite different, schools of philosophy: Kantian dualism and Spinozan monism.

Immanuel Kant, in grappling with the rational metaphysics of the eighteenth century, was shaken from his 'slumbers' by David Hume's attack on metaphysics in *An Inquiry Concerning Human Understanding*. In Hume's words:

---

1. Macfarlane, 'Remarks on the Times', *Democratic Review*, May 1850, See p. 6 below.
2. Ibid.

If we take in our hand any volume of divinity or school metaphysics, for instance let us ask, Does it contain any abstract reasoning concerning quantity or number? No. Does it contain any experimental reasoning concerning matter of fact and existence? No. Commit it then to the flames for it can contain nothing but sophistry and illusion.[1]

Hume's critique of metaphysics is accepted by Kant as a decisive refutation of the idea that the universal forms and categories of reason can be grounded in the external world as experienced through the senses by means of inductive logic. But Kant then turns the table on the empiricists with his argument that the universals are *a priori* to sensuous experience. Summarizing Kant's 'Revolution', Heinrich Heine (a student of Hegel much admired by Macfarlane) writes irreverently:

Once upon a time Reason, like a sun, circled around the world of appearances, and sought to illuminate it; but Kant bade Reason to stand still and now the world of appearance revolves around and is illumined by it...[2]

Although Kant denies that there are any *a priori*—or factual—grounds for religious belief, he does allow for the idea of a *"moral governor of the world"* as a *postulate* of practical reason. Without this postulate, he argues, the will of the acting moral subject would have no definite object and would be left only with the empty forms of the law: *"It concerns us not so much to know what God is in Himself (his nature), as what he is for us as moral beings..."*[3]

According to René Descartes, the difference between the 'inner' and 'outer' world of experience is essentially the difference between substance as thought—indivisible consciousness—and substance as matter—divisible in its three-dimensional 'extensions'; and although both are divine creations, they are quite separate spheres of substance. Baruch Spinoza, whilst appropriating the dualist Cartesian categories, developed a *monist* philosophy, which denies that there is any such world of ideas, forms or eter-

---

1. David Hume, *An Inquiry Concerning Human Understanding*. Oxford: Clarendon Press, 1975, p. 165.
2. Heinrich Heine, *Self Portrait and Other Prose Writings*, Secaucus 1948, p. 465.
3. Immanuel Kant, *Religion Within the Limits of Reason Alone*, New York: Harper and Row, 1960, p. 130.

nal moral truths existing separately from the world of natural objects. In Spinoza's writings, the terms 'God' and 'Nature' are interchangeable; and thought and extensions of thought are understood as essential *attributes* of an infinite, absolute and self-manifesting substance. The physical shapes of all natural objects in the universe are modifications—or 'modes'—of the universal attribute of three-dimensionality. Thus humans, as natural beings, are modes of divine attributes in a physical sense, but also in the 'spiritual' sense: the derived modes of the attribute of thought are manifested in the 'pure' universal truths of science, mathematics, philosophy, and the like. All individual things can be referred back to the One Substance that is the 'inner cause' of everything.

In German idealism the Spinozist concept of substance had the effect of radicalising the 'active' part of the Kantian philosophy, i.e., the *transcendental ego*. The post-Kantian philosophy of Johann Gottlieb Fichte, conceives of an 'Absolute Self', equivalent to Spinoza's 'Absolute Substance', which contains all reality and has nothing outside of itself. In 1795, under Fichte's influence, the poet Friedrich Hölderlin, writes to Hegel:

> *There is no object for this absolute self, since otherwise all reality would not be in it. Yet a consciousness without an object is inconceivable... Thus in the Absolute Self no self-consciousness is conceivable; as Absolute Self I have no self-consciousness.*[1]

At the same time, Friedrich Wilhelm Schelling, also in a letter to Hegel, presses home the same point:

> *For Spinoza the world, the object by itself in opposition to the subject, was everything, for me it is the self... There is no supersensible world for us than that of the Absolute Self. God is nothing but the Absolute Self... personality arises through the unity of consciousness. Yet consciousness is not possible without an object. But for God—i.e. the Absolute Self—there is no possible object whatsoever, for if there was the Absolute Self would cease to be absolute. Consequently, there is no personal God.*[2]

Hegel, like these young philosophic comrades, breaks decisively with Theism, as when he calls for *"Absolute freedom of all spirits*

---

1. Quoted in Merold Westphal, 'Hegel and Onto-Theology', *Hegel Society of Great Britain Bulletin*, 41/42, 2000.
2. Quoted in Merold Westphal, op cit.

who bear the intellectual world in themselves, and cannot seek either God or immortality outside themselves". Hegel recognizes Spinoza's idea of 'substance' as the *"abstract unity which mind is in itself"* and as the essential beginning of *all* philosophy; a restatement of the pre-Socratic idea of Being first formulated by Anaxagoras and Parmenides:

> *when man begins to philosophize, the soul must commence by bathing in this ether of the One Substance, in which all that man has held as true has disappeared; this negation of all that is particular... is the liberation of the mind and its absolute foundation.*[1]

Hegel sees Spinoza's abolition of the modern Cartesian separation of corporeality and the thinking 'I' as *"in the main true and well-grounded"*. Hegel however, thinks that in Spinoza's conception the individual merely *"enters into external existence with what is 'other'"*, and is trapped in a *"false individuality"* which lacks the subjectivity of Being-for-self, and thus vanishes into existence without a *"return"* to the universal. The individual, lacking the *"principle of personality"*, is left homeless and does not *"rise"* through the particular to the unity of the Concept. *Substance*, for Hegel, is also *subject*. Whereas Spinoza's negation is infinite, Hegel's 'absolute negativity' represents at the same time the 'negation of the negation', working through history and philosophy. Hegel sees the beginnings of Absolute Ethical Life in the lost 'organic' unity of the city-state in Greek Antiquity and sees the potential of freedom in the modern world as limited by the relativised ethical life of bourgeois property relations, which reaches its philosophic limits in the abstract categorical imperatives of Kantian dualism.[2]

Hegel's *Philosophy of Religion* (1827) sees the religious *"form of representation"* as having been a historical necessity for making Christian doctrine universally accessible to the masses through the medium of the church. But since the domain of this representation is the world of the past, its spiritual being is only implicit; it lacks the *"absolute singularity of presence to self"*. In Hegel's view, Biblical and church history must not be allowed to rule over the present or determine the future. The inwardising movement of self-consciousness can only take place through the *"return from appearance"* to the Concept, i.e. through the thinking reason of

---

1. Ibid.
2. Gillian Rose, *Hegel Contra Sociology*, London: 1981.

the free spirit, which, following its adventures through the kingdom of 'naïve religion', the republic of the materialist Enlightenment, and the 'third estate' and the 'community of philosophy', returns into the *"inner place of the community and its organisation"*.[1]

But how was the Christian 'community', fed sagas about the Devil, miracles and the like, to be raised towards the absolute of philosophical reason? If the form of religious representation expressed a content—the gospels—whose facticity could not stand up to historical criticism, then how could the form be reconciled with any true inwardisation? These were the questions posed by the young Left Hegelian, David Strauss, who sought to answer them by taking Hegel's insights further. Just as for Hegel the given immediacy grasped through sense-certainty was only the first moment of dialectical philosophy, so for Strauss, the immediacy of religious consciousness through *"dogma or sacred history"* had to undergo the negative mediation of free historical criticism. For Strauss, the Christian absolute of the incarnation was contradictory because, restricted as it was to one individual (Jesus), it lacked the inclusivity of a real absolute. Strauss's *The Life of Jesus, Critically Examined* (1835-36) argues: *"It is humanity that dies, rises and ascends to heaven, for from the negation of its phenomenal life there ever proceeds a higher spiritual life"*. The legacy of the Christian mythos of resurrection is that *"from the kindling within him of the idea of humanity the individual man participates in the divine life of the species"*, and the rational subject and historical substance are united in the cause of progress.[2]

In Helen Macfarlane's writings of 1850, which show a definite Straussian influence, such unity means recognizing that *"the days of orthodox Protestantism are numbered"*:

> *The human mind has not been standing still for the last 300 years. Men are beginning to perceive that this system satisfies neither the heart nor the head; neither the imagination or the intellect. For it swept away all the poetry of the Christian Mythos and gave a death blow to the art of the middle ages. It left us with nothing but a set of abstract creeds and dogmas professedly based*

---

1. Hegel, *Philosophy of Religion*, Section in part 3 on 'Christianity as the Consummate Religion', in *G.W.F. Hegel: Theologian of the Spirit*, ed. P. Hodgson, Nashville: Fortress Press, 1993.
2. Marilyn Chapin Massey, 'The Literature of Young Germany and D. F. Strauss's *Life of Jesus*', *The Journal of Religion*, Vol. 59, No. 3, July 1979.

upon another set of questionable sagas and hearsays... scholastic formulas; which... have been outgrown... and are now so many impediments [to] spiritual development... what is the meaning of Protestantism? It is a state of transition. It is the stepping stone for the human mind in its progress from deism to pantheism—that is, from a belief in some things, in the divinity of one being or of one man, to a belief in the divinity of All beings, of All men—in the holiness of All things...[1]

Ten years earlier, in 1839, the young Friedrich Engels (still not yet a socialist or atheist) had, in breaking with Protestantism, declared his conversion to Strauss's Hegelian 'pantheism':

Through Strauss I have now entered on the straight road to Hegelianism. Of course, I shall not become such an inveterate Hegelian... but I must nevertheless absorb important things from this colossal system. The Hegelian idea of God has already become mine, and thus I am joining the ranks of the 'modern pantheists'... knowing well that even the word pantheism arouses such colossal revulsion on the part of pastors who don't think... Modern pantheism, i.e., Hegel, apart from the fact that it is already found among the Chinese and Parsees, is perfectly expressed in the sect of the Libertines, which was attacked by Calvin. This discovery is really rather too original. But still more original is its development.[2]

Strauss follows Hegel in showing that implicitly, the thought content of religion had an objective, theoretical drive. The difference is that for Hegel, the importance of the gospels was their symbolic content rather than their historicity, whereas for Strauss the gospel narratives were myths, which had preserved and translated the Messianic desires of the early Christian communities.[3] In the early 1840s, Strauss came under attack from the atheist Ludwig Feuerbach and his supporters for being too Hegelian. Feuerbach argued that there was nothing objective to be found in theological knowledge; all of which, he argued, contained only subjective yearnings and projections of human suf-

---

1. Macfarlane, 'Red Stockings and Lawn Sleeves', *Friend of the People*, 21 and 26 December 1850.

2. Engels to Friedrich Graeber, 21 December 1839. *Marx and Engels Collected Works, Volume 2*, p. 487.

3. David McLellan, *Marx Before Marxism*, London: 1970, pp. 21-23.

Ludwig Feuerbach

David Strauss

fering.[1] According to Feuerbach's *Essence of Christianity*, "*God as God is the sum of all human perfection; God as Christ is the sum of all human misery*". The Christian doctrine of the incarnation of God represents love in a human form: "*Love attests itself by suffering*".[2] Although the young Engels embraced Feuerbach's atheism as an advance on Strauss's 'pantheism', Engels later highlighted some of Feuerbach's shortcomings in comparison with Hegel:

> *With Hegel evil is the form in which the motive force of historical development is presented. This has a twofold meaning. On the one hand, each new advance necessarily appears as a sacrilege against things hallowed, as a rebellion against conditions which are old and moribund but sanctified by custom; on the other hand, it is precisely men's wicked passions, greed and lust for power, which, with the emergence of class antagonisms, serve as levers of historical development, a fact of which the history of feudalism and of the bourgeoisie, for example, constitutes a single continual proof. But it does not occur to Feuerbach to investigate the historical role of moral evil. To him history is altogether a weird and dismal hell.*[3]

For Feuerbach, the genesis of religious symbols was best explained by sciences of human subjectivity such as psychology and anthropology, and in human needs and wants. Contrary to the whole tradition of modern philosophy from Descartes to Hegel, Feuerbach—and this explains his appeal to vulgar-materialist 'Marxists'—conceives of the ego as passive and determined by 'objective' reality, rather than as spontaneous and active. Against Hegel's view that truth is a universal that cannot be grasped purely from sense-perception of particulars, Feuerbach upholds sense-certainty as the final criterion of the truth. According to Herbert Marcuse, "*This is the point in which Marx's critique of Feuerbach begins*", a point at which "*Marx upholds Hegel as against Feuerbach... truth finds its fulfilment in a historical process carried forward by the collective practice of men*".[4] As Marx argues:

---

1. Marilyn Chapin Massey, 'David Friedrich Strauss and His Hegelian Critics', *The Journal of Religion*, Vol. 57, No. 4, October 1977.
2. Ludwig Feuerbach, *The Essence of Christianity*, New York: Dover, 2008, pp. 28, 37.
3. Engels, *Ludwig Feuerbach and the End of Classical German Philosophy*, section III.
4. Herbert Marcuse, *Reason and Revolution*, 1941, p. 271.

> *Feuerbach resolves the religious essence into the human essence. But the human essence is no abstraction in each single individual. In its reality it is the ensemble of the social relations.*[1]

Macfarlane may well have read Marx's article, 'Critique of Hegel's Philosophy of Right: Introduction', published in the *Deutsch-Französische Jahrbücher*, in February 1844. Regarding the "*demand*" of the "*practical political party in Germany*" for "*the negation of philosophy*", the young Marx writes:

> *Where it goes wrong is in limiting itself to a demand which it does not and cannot achieve. It believes that it can carry out this negation by turning its back on philosophy and mumbling a few irritable and banal phrases over its shoulder at it... You demand that we make the real seeds of life our point of departure, but you forget that the real seeds of life embryo of the German people has up to now only flourished inside its cranium. In a word: You cannot transcend philosophy without realizing it. The same mistake, but with the factors reversed, was made by the theoretical political party, which has its origins in philosophy.*[2]

The young Marx has very little to say about Strauss (*"still, at least implicitly, imprisoned within Hegelian logic"*[3]) and undoubtedly sees Feuerbach's criticisms of Hegelian philosophy as deeper and more advanced (also, the issues were political as well as philosophical: Feuerbach declared himself as a 'communist'—though in a vague, ill-defined sense—whereas Strauss did not). What is certain is that Marx did not follow Feuerbach in dismissing Hegel's concept of the negation of the negation. Feuerbach sees Hegel's 'negation of the negation' as a dialectical contradiction of philosophy with itself: the idea produces reality which it then absorbs back into itself as 'self-consciousness' (this, in contrast to Strauss, who sees the Christian religion as in contradiction with its divine, pantheistic essence—a contradiction that can be overcome by means of the dialectical insights gained from Hegel's

---

1. Karl Marx, *The German Ideology*, Sixth Theses on Feuerbach', http://www.marxists.org/archive/marx/works/1845/theses/index.htm.
2. Marx, *Early Writings*, London, 1975, pp. 249-50
3. Marx, 'Critique of Hegel's Dialectic and General Philosophy', *Early Writings*, p. 380. See also, Marx, 'Luther as Arbiter between Strauss and Feuerbach', in *Writings of the Young Marx on Philosophy and Society*, New York, 1967, pp. 93-95.

philosophy). In any case, Marx sees in Hegel's absolute negativity what Feuerbach does not:

> The importance of Hegel's Phenomenology and its final result—the dialectic of negativity as the moving and producing principle—lies in the fact that Hegel conceives the self-creation of man as a process, objectification as loss of object, as alienation and as supersession of this alienation; so that he therefore grasps the nature of labour and conceives objective man—true, because real man—as the result of his own labour.[1]

Helen Macfarlane's writings suggest that, in engaging with the ideas of Marx and Engels, she did not feel the need to approach them through the *"weird and dismal hell"* a Feuerbachian makes of actual history; rather, she got there by radicalizing Strauss's critical Hegelianism. When Strauss's *The Life of Jesus Critically Examined* was translated into English in 1846 by Marian Evans (George Eliot), it was described as *"the most pestilential book ever vomited out of the jaws of hell"* by Lord Ashley, Earl of Shaftesbury, a leading Anglican Evangelical whose speeches in the House of Lords were much ridiculed by Macfarlane. Like so many others of the Hegelian Left, Strauss did not embrace socialism. But for Macfarlane, what Strauss called the *"divine life of the species"* could hardly be anything else.

Why a 'hobgoblin'?

> *Ein Gespenst geht um in Europa—des Gespenst des Kommunismus.*
> **Marx and Engels**, *Communist Manifesto* (1848)
>
> *A spectre is haunting Europe. The spectre of Communism.*
> **Samuel Moore**, translation (1888)
>
> *A frightful hobgoblin stalks throughout Europe. We are haunted by a ghost. The ghost of Communism.*
> **Herlen Macfarlane**, translation (1850)

Why a Hobgoblin? Many of today's leftist cognoscenti see Macfarlane's use of the 'frightful Hobgoblin' as somewhat comical. In 1850 however, it would have been taken as sound literary currency. 'Hobgoblin' occurs in a famous essay by the American Transcendentalist philosopher, Ralph Waldo Emerson, who was

---

1. Marx, *Early Writings*, pp. 385-86.

evidently one of Macfarlane's favourite writers. Emerson writes in *Self-Reliance*:

> *The other terror that scares us from self-trust is our consistency; a reverence for our past act or word, because the eyes of others have no other data for computing our orbit than our past acts, and we are loath to disappoint them... In your metaphysics you have denied personality to the Deity: yet when the devout motions of the soul come, yield to them heart and life, though they should clothe God with shape and color. Leave your theory, as Joseph his coat in the hand of the harlot, and flee. A foolish consistency is the* **hobgoblin** *of little minds, adored by little statesmen and philosophers and divines.*[1]

Another possible source, suggested by Louise Yeoman, is Jeremy Bentham's chapter in the *Book of Fallacies* (1824), entitled 'The Hobgoblin Argument, or, No Innovation'.

> *The,* **hobgoblin,** *the eventual appearance of which is denounced by this argument, is anarchy which tremendous spectre has for its forerunner innovation... 'Here it comes!' exclaims the barbarous and unthinking servant in the hearing of the afrighted child, when to rid herself of the burden of attendance... the effects of which may continue during life. 'Here it comes!' is the cry. And the* **hobgoblin** *is rendered all the more terrific by the suppression of its name. Of a similar nature and productive of similar effects is the political device here exposed to view...*

The 'device' sees *"bad motives, bad designs, bad conduct and character"* in those advocating change. But, as Bentham points out:

> *Whatever is now established, was once innovation... he condemns the Revolution, the Reformation, the assumption made by the House of Commons of a part in the pennings of the law... All these he bids us regard as forerunners of the monster anarchy.*[2]

Macfarlane seems to echo this line of thought when she writes of Democracy as *"the nightmare and old bogy"* of all 'respectable formalists', who always ask, *"what will people say of it? Not, is it true? Is it right?"*[3] However, as she sees democratic communism as the

---
1. Ralph Waldo Emerson, 'Self-Reliance', *Essays: New Series*, 1841.
2. Jeremy Bentham and Sir John Bowring, *The Works of Jeremy Bentham*, London 1843.
3. Helen Macfarlane, 'Democracy'.

very essence of the required 'change' Bentham's opponents are arguing against, Macfarlane—contra Bentham—is evoking a *real* hobgoblin to terrify the established order.

It has been noted that in modern music, 'bands tend to grow into their names'.[1] Similarly do concepts—like 'Hobgoblin' or 'Spectre' (or consider Guy Debord's 'Spectacle')—as evoked in revolutionary literature. On this phenomenon we might take note of some relevant remarks by Manuel Yang, in his writings on the poet and philosopher, Taka'aki Yoshimoto (1924-2012). Like E.P. Thompson in *The Making of the English Working Class*, Yoshimoto refuses to dissolve the masses' lived actions and consciousness into sociological 'structures' prescribed by intellectuals. Like Marx, he rejects the 'communal illusion' of the state, which he believes the post-war Japanese Left failed to shake off. Manuel Yang, for his part, wants to rethink Marx, Yoshimoto and Thompson through the perspective of struggles over the 'commons'. In doing so, Yang refers to my observation on Macfarlane's 'Hobgoblin':

> *Macfarlane, translating the* Communist Manifesto, *tries to give 'Ein Gespenst' a double meaning. It is not just the ghostly apparition that haunts the castles of Shakespeare's* Macbeth *and* Hamlet, *foretelling doom and retribution for the incumbents. It is also the scary sprite that country folks tell their children lurks in the woods, in order to discourage them from wandering off on their own.*[2]

Yang comments on this:

> *Indeed hobgoblins, which belong to the historical imaginary of the Scottish fairyland, are creatures that inhabit the daily world of peasant communing. This world had ready access to demotic curses, often expressed in such fairy tales and premised on customary laws that were intended to protect traditional popular rights from the cupidity of self-interest, the central tenet of bour-*

---

1. A remark made by guitarist Simon King when he was part of Kenny Process Team, during a conversation in their Forest Gate house conducted by Ben Watson to draw attention to their astonishing LP *Surfin' With* (Heniola, 1994).
2. David Black, *Helen Macfarlane*, p. 94.

geois rationality, whose bloody acts of exorcism took the form of enclosures, privatization, imperialism.[1]

Yang quotes from Henderson and Cowan's *Scottish Fairy Belief* (2001):

Fairies were firmly connected to the landscape and deeply rooted in the soil. The importance of respecting the land which they frequented was widely recognized. It was bad luck to interfere with, or try to remove, trees, bushes, stones, ancient buildings or anything else believed to have fairy associations. Misfortune, illness, or even death might result from tampering with fairy property.[2]

In a similar vein, Peter Linebaugh writes:

'Hob' was the name of a country labourer, 'goblin' a mischievous sprite. Thus communism manifested itself in the Manifesto *in the discourse of the agrarian commons. The substrate of the language revealing the imprint of the clouted shoon*[3] *in the sixteenth century who fought to have all things in common. The trajectory from commons to communism can be cast as passage from past to future. For Marx personally it corresponded to his intellectual progress. The criminalization of the woodland of the Moselle Valley peasantry provided him with his first experience with economic questions...*[4]

Although historical evidence to connect Scottish fairy belief with any actual struggles against bourgeois encroachment on common land would seem to be lacking, Yang's recognition of historical objectivity in Hegel's 'idealist' concepts is Macfarlane-like. Comparing 'Spectre' to 'Hobgoblin', he writes:

If 'spectre' is a more philosophically mediated, reified form, divorced from the earthly spirits that directly haunt the peasant imagination, its Hegelian origin nonetheless lay in the commons, as Marx recognized with genuine surprise twenty years after com-

---

1. Manuel Yang, PhD paper, *Yoshimoto Taka'aki, Communal Illusion, and the Japanese New Left*: http://www.ohiolink.edu/etd/send-pdf.cgi?toledo1122656731
2. Lizanne Henderson and Edward Cowan, *Scottish Fairy Belief: A History*, East Linton: Tuckwell Press, 2000.
3. A shoe tipped with iron toecaps.
4. Peter Linebaugh, 'Karl Marx, the Theft of Wood, Working Class Composition', *Crime and Social Justice*, No. #6 (Autumn-Winter 1976).

posing the Manifesto [*in his* Pre-capitalist Economic Formations, *p 142*]: "But what would old Hegel say in the next world if he heard that the general, [*Allgemaine*], in German and Norse means but the common land [*Gemeinland*], and the particular, [*Sundre, Besondere*], nothing but the separate property divided off from the common land?"[1]

Helen Macfarlane's break with George Julian Harney

December 31st 1850, Harney is throwing a party on behalf of the Fraternal Democrats at the London Literary and Scientific Institute in John Street, near the Tottenham Court Road. Present are numerous London Chartists and exiled revolutionaries from various countries, including the German Communists, Karl Marx, Friedrich Engels and Karl Schapper. Women known to be present are Jenny Marx, Helen Macfarlane and Harney's wife, Mary. It is not a happy occasion. Harney makes a speech on the political situation at home and abroad over the last year. He says that there has been *"little cause for encouragement"*, because *"nowhere have the people become possessed of institutions which could alone ensure their prosperity in return for their toil"*. Engels also makes a speech. The failures of the European Revolutions and consequent reaction had been due to *"the ignorance of the people and the treachery of their leaders"*. The revolution, he says, will only come again after *"a long struggle, consummated by a new generation of men"*.[2]

Earlier in the year, Marx and Engels' Communist League had been negotiating with the Fraternal Democrats and the French Blanquists to form a 'World League of Revolutionary Socialists'. During that period that Marx developed the perspective of 'Revolution in Permanence', arguing that, although revolutionary workers' parties could and would march with the petit-bourgeois radicals against the reactionary enemy, they would have to oppose all attempts by the radicals to consolidate their position to the detriment of the workers. The plan for the World League

---

1. These politics will come as no surprise to fans of Japanese animation film studio, Studio Ghibli. See, e.g., *My Neighbour Totoro* (1988), *Pom Poko* (1994) and *Spirited Away* (2001).
2. *Northern Star*, 4 Jan, 1851.

came unstuck when some of those involved, including Harney and Schapper, were drawn towards unity with another body called the 'Central European Democratic Committee'. This had been formed by the moderate French socialist, Louis Blanc, the Italian nationalist Guiseppe Mazzini, and Marx's erstwhile collaborator in Germany, Arnold Ruge. In appealing for an immediate revival of the defeated European Revolutions, the Committee rejected *"the cold and unfeeling travail of the intellect"* in favour of the *"instinct of the masses"* as *"the people in motion"*. To Marx's mind this was tantamount to demanding that the people *"have no thought for the morrow and must strike all ideas from the mind"* and that *"the riddle of the future will be solved by a miracle"*.[1] Schapper *"demanded, if not real conspiracies, at least the appearance of conspiracies, and accordingly favoured an alliance with the heroes of the hour"*.[2] At the September 15th London meeting of the central authority of the Communist League, Marx said of Schapper's proposals to unite with the Committee:

> *The revolution is not seen as a product of the realities of the situation but as the result of an effort of will. Whereas we say to the workers: you have 15, 20, 50 years of civil war to go through in order to alter the situation and to train yourselves for the exercise of power it is said: we must take power at once, or else we might as well take to our beds. Just as the democrats abused the word 'people' so now the word 'proletariat' has been used as a mere phrase.*[3]

The debate split the League and ended the efforts to build the World League of Revolutionary Socialists. But Harney's enthusiasm for organizing banquets and rallies in the name of international brotherhood was undiminished. His efforts drew scorn from Marx, who referred to Harney as 'Mr Hippipharra'.

To add to the political tensions of the year 1850, there has been a lot of stress in the Marx household. Karl and Jenny are mourning the death of their one-year old son Heinrich six weeks earlier. In August, Jenny, pregnant again, had undertaken a trip to Holland on a desperate and fruitless mission to get money from an uncle to help feed their three surviving children and pay the mounting rent arrears for their Dean Street lodgings. While

---

1. Marx and Engels, *Collected Works*, Vol 10, pp. 529-31.
2. Marx, *Herr Vogt*, London: New Park, 1982, p. 28.
3. MECW, Vol 10, pp. 626-8.

she was away Marx had an affair with their German housekeeper, Helene 'Lenchen' Demuth. As a result Lenchen too is pregnant and Marx is worried about his factional opponents *"disseminating the most unspeakable infamies about me"*. Jenny, he tells Engels, is suffering from *"the most disagreeable of domestic quandaries"*, as well as *"exhalations from the pestiferous democratic cloaca"* and *"stupid tell-tales"*.[1] The stress Marx must have been under might explain his harsh and slightly 'paranoid' tone concerning Mary Harney in a letter to Engels some weeks later on the subject of the New Years Eve event. Marx says Mary, whilst having a great partiality for Louis Blanc, Karl Schapper and his collaborator, the dashing Prussian ex-cavalry lieutenant, August Willich,

> *hates me as a frivolous person who might become dangerous to her "property to be watched upon". I have definite proof that this woman has got her too long plebeian fingers in the pie here. How much Harney is possessed by this familiar spirit and how sly and narrowly Scots she is you can judge from the following. You will remember how on New Year's Eve, she insulted Helen Macfarlane in the presence of my wife. Later she told my wife with a smiling face that Harney hadn't seen Miss Macfarlane for the whole evening. Later she told him that she had declined her acquaintanceship because the cleft dragoon had evoked the dismay and ridicule of the whole company and of my wife in particular. Harney was stupid and cowardly enough not to let her get her own back for the insult, and so break, in the most undignified way, with the only collaborator on his spouting rag who had original ideas—a rare bird, on his paper...*[2]

Thus ended Helen Macfarlane's collaboration with George Julian Harney, the Fraternal Democrats and the ailing, doomed Chartist movement. In April 1851, Harney's *Friend of the People* mentioned *"H. Morton's fundraising efforts for the Polish and Hungarian refugees in Liverpool threatened with deportation"*. The defeated survivors of the revolutionary Polish Legion had sailed to Liverpool, and were seeking asylum. The British government, it later turned out, not wishing to welcome revolutionary 'aliens', utilized secret

---

1. Francis Wheen, *Karl Marx*, London: Fourth Estate, 1999, pp. 171-6.
2. Marx to Engels, 23 February 1851. MECW Vol 38, p. 291. I have used Schoyen's translation, *Chartist Challenge*, p. 215.

service money to pay for their passage to America.[1] The Chartist *Northern Star* for 5 April 1851 lists 'Miss Helen Macfarlane' as having contributed 10 shillings to the National Charter Association. After this, Helen Macfarlane, along with 'Howard Morton' disappears from the surviving records of the Chartist movement.

After Chartism—travels and tragedy

New research by Louise Yeoman, Shelagh Spenser and myself has revealed what happened to Helen Macfarlane subsequently. The first clue is in the passage from Marx just quoted:

> *[Mary Harney] told my wife with a smiling face that Harney hadn't seen Miss Macfarlane for the whole evening. Later she told him that she had declined her acquaintanceship because the cleft dragoon had evoked the dismay and ridicule of the whole company and of my wife in particular.*

This hints that Miss Macfarlane was in the company of the man Marx calls the 'cleft dragoon', and that he may have been of military background and bearing a duelling scar. It also indicates that the comrade was not, for whatever reason, in 'very good shape' mentally. We now know that in late-1851 or thereabouts Helen Macfarlane married one Francis Proust, 'late of Brussels', and that in 1852 she gave birth to a daughter they named Consuela Pauline Roland Proust (Consuela after the heroine of the George Sands novel serialised in Harney's paper, and Pauline Roland after the imprisoned and martyred French socialist feminist thinker, 1805–52). Having started a family, they decided, in 1852, to emigrate to Natal, South Africa. Following the forced annexation by the British of the Boer Republic of Natalia in 1843, merchant land speculators, governmental 'Colonial Reformers' and Christian co-operators joined forces to recruit emigrants into a scheme for establishing arable farming communities. The Natal Emigration and Colonization Company's Manchester agent was Helen Macfarlane's brother John. After the collapse of Feargus O'Connor's scheme to resettle urban workers in co-operative freeholdings (the 'Land Plan'), the Natal scheme may have had some appeal as a benevolent and socially innovative attempt to establish a new English yeomanry in a new land,

---

1. Schoyen, p. 212. See also Bernard Porter, *The Refugee Question in Victorian Politics*, Cambridge: CUP, 1979.

free of industrial depredation and corruption. Five of Helen's brothers and one of her sisters were among the 7,500 British emigrants who took the voyage to Natal in the years 1849–52. By 1853 Pietermaritzburg, where the Macfarlanes settled, was *"a tranquil, pleasant place in its setting of hills. The market square was the centre... The people of Pietermaritzburg built attractive homes with thatched roofs. Water furrows lined the streets"*.[1]

At the end of 1852, Helen, husband and child boarded the 'Lady of the Lake', at the Port of London, bound for Natal. The ship, an old wooden-hulled sailing barque, would have made for an uncomfortable voyage in rough seas and bad weather. According to later reports in the Natal press, Helen arrived at Durban on 28 March 1853 with her daughter, but without her husband. It was reported that Francis Proust had left the ship at Deal (on the English Channel) because he was too sick to continue the voyage. This is distinctly odd. Deal was *not* a port-of-call for ships on oceanic passages. And what kind of state would a husband have to be in to leave his wife and child to continue an arduous and dangerous three-month voyage without him? Could his illness have been mental as well as physical? Could the story of him ever boarding even have been some sort of fabrication on behalf of the Macfarlane family, if not Helen herself, to cover up his disappearance? In any event, for Helen, worse was to come. Days after arriving in Natal, Consuela died at McDonald's Hotel, Durban.

By the time Helen Proust arrived in Natal, the settler schemes for arable farming were failing (the land had previously supported the pastoral farming of the Boers, but proved to be unsuitable for arable cultivation). After a stay in Natal for one year and three months, she returned to England. On 21 June 1854 she sailed on the 'Gitana' for Cape Town, on the first leg of a long and lonely voyage back to England, by which time she would have known that Francis Proust had died. Arriving back in England in September 1854, Helen moved in with her unmarried elder sister Agnes at Tynwald Terrace, in Manchester's Moss Side, just 200 yards from the lodging house at Moss Lane East where Friedrich Engels lived with his lover, Mary Burns and her sister Lizzie from 1855 to 1859. If Helen was still associated

---

1. I. M. Birkett, 'The Heritage from Mr W. L. Howes JP. of his Personal Experiences of Old Natal': *http://salbu.co.za/debora/Howes2.html*.

with Engels, there could be an interesting connection with what happened next in her life. For Engels was a keen fox-hunter and a member of the Cheshire Hunt; and in the area where the Cheshire Hunt took place lies the sleepy, leafy parish of Baddiley, just outside Nantwich. At some point after her return to England, in 1854, Helen met Church of England Reverend John Wilkinson Edwards of St. Michaels Church, Baddiley, himself recently widowed with a family of 11 children. Edwards has left no writings with which to ascertain any definite political or theological views he had. However, evidence unearthed by Louise Yeoman shows that when Edwards graduated from Oxford, his first incumbency at the Lancashire parish of Astley, from 1837 to 1840 caused some consternation among Anglican 'traditionalists'. According to the memoirs of one Reverend Hewlett, Edwards made radical changes in the Astley parish Sunday school which were connected with 'political agitation' in the neighbourhood. This was at a time when Chartist activity was at its height, and when there was a significant Chartist presence in Astley. If Rev. John Wilkinson Edwards had a professional tendency to 'stir things up' then he had at least that in common with Helen Proust, née Macfarlane. What Edwards and Helen Proust certainly had in common was class status and level of education, but perhaps more importantly, bereavement. In 1856 they married. Ironically then, Helen Macfarlane, who fulminated in her writings against the Anglican church (and organised religion generally), finally embraced it. One might speculate that Helen's reconversion to church-going Christianity shared something in common with the reconversion of Marian Evans, with whom she had much in common. Evans, at the age of 22, had defied her parents and refused to go to church, saying of the Bible:

> *I regard these writings as histories consisting of mingled truth and fiction, and while I admire and cherish much of what I believe to have been the moral teaching of Jesus himself, I consider the system of doctrines built upon the facts of his life... to be most dishonourable to God and most pernicious in its influence on individual and social happiness.*[1]

Later, Evans returned to the Church, because she found the Feuerbachian positivism of 'speculative truth' and 'agreement be-

---
1. Quoted in Kathryn Hughes, *George Eliot: The Last Victorian*, New York, 2001, pp. 50-51.

tween intellects' as lacking "*the truth of feeling as the only universal bond of union*"; having decided that it was impossible to "*wrench*" away the "*intellectual errors*" of the believer without destroying his or her "*vitality*".[1] Evans's studies of German critical philosophy had never, however, led her to merge secularized Christianity with Communism, as did Macfarlane before she settled for the domestic simplicity of being a vicar's wife.

Helen Edwards gave birth to two sons, Herbert and Walter. She didn't enjoy her quiet life for very long however. At the age of only 41, she fell ill with bronchitis and died. She is buried in the churchyard of St. Michaels. The inscription on the gravestone reads: "*Sacred to the memory of Helen, wife of the Rev. John W. Edwards, who fell asleep in Jesus, March the 29th 1860, aged 41 years. 'So he giveth his beloved sleep'*".

David Black, 30-*xii*-2014

---

1. Ibid., p. 55.

Democratic Review

April 1850 to September 1850

Remarks on the Times—
Apropos of Certain Passages in No. I of Thomas Carlyle's Latter-day Pamphlets

Democratic Review, **April, May and June 1850**

Part one

It appears to me that my illustrious countryman, while writing this pamphlet, has been rough ridden by an idea, and has concentrated his attention on one aspect of truth, to the exclusion of all other aspects of the same. The impression left on my mind by the perusal of this pamphlet is, that Mr Carlyle distrusts the tendency of the present age; his artistic temperament cannot endure the ruin and decay to which society in Europe is fast hastening. Perhaps, like Goethe, he would go the length of preferring injustice to confusion.[1] Well, for choice, I would rather be an architect than a scavenger; it is better to build up than to pull down and sweep away. Yet the scavenger is a very useful kind of

---

1. Although Johann Wolfgang von Goethe (1749–1832) regarded himself as neither a revolutionary nor a reactionary, he pronounced after the victory of the French revolutionary forces at the Battle of Valmy in 1792, *"Here, today, a new epoch in world history has begun, and you can say that you were present."* In 1793, Goethe was present at the Siege of Mainz when, under bombardment by Austrian and Prussian armies, the French negotiated an evacuation of their troops and German republicans. When a mob attempted to lynch one of the departing Germans, Goethe intervened physically and rescued him. Asked why he had done so, he replied, *"It is simply my nature—I would rather commit an injustice than tolerate disorder."* (Peter Boerner, *Goethe*, Haus Publishing, 2005, pp. 64-8)

person. So is the destructive, the go-ahead radical of the present day.[1] There is a want of consistency in Mr Carlyle, admitting that *democracy is the Fact of the present age*, and then denying that democracy is *possible*, because the world has never yet seen a democracy.[2] Well, what then? Because a thing is new, does it follow that it is impossible? The world has never yet seen a democratic form of society, for the simple reason, that democracy is the Ultimate Fact of the present time, and not that of any other time. Not even in America?—asks a reader. I answer, decidedly not. There are two facts existing in that country—to me they are very disgusting facts—which are as much opposed to the democratic idea, as any Institution in the old world. American negro slavery, and American exclusion of white women from the exercise of all political, and many social, rights—are things as much opposed

---

1. In 1833, *The Poor Man's Guardian* was prosecuted by the Liberal government because its publisher, Henry Hetherington (1792–1849), refused to pay the Newspaper Stamp Tax, popularly known as the 'Knowledge Tax'. Hetherington defiantly launched a new paper, provocatively titled *The Destructive*, for which he was again prosecuted.
2. Thomas Carlyle (1795-1881) portrayed the mediaeval monastery of St. Edmundsbury as exemplifying the rule of a 'real aristocracy' over contented serfs. In contrast, Victorian England was under the sway of a 'sham aristocracy', much inferior to the 'real aristocracy' of the 'Captains of Industry'. Carlyle supported the New Poor Law of 1834 as a means to 'encourage' the 'surplus population' to emigrate: "*If paupers are made miserable, paupers will needs decline in multitude. It is a secret known to all rat catchers…*" (Carlyle, *Critical and Miscellaneous Essays IV*, London: 1872, p. 130.) In invoking the 'Spirit of 1066', he compared the Norman barbarians to "*an immense volunteer police force, stationed everywhere, united disciplined, feudally regimented, ready for action; strong Teutonic men…*" (p. 189) It is hardly surprising, given his lethal attitude to the victims of capitalism, that in the twentieth century Carlyle became the Nazis' favourite British writer:

> Between Black West Indians and our own White Ireland, between these two extremes of lazy refusal to work… and of inability to find any work…

Carlyle called for a 'regiment' of the unemployed to be set to work on the land:

> Refuse to strike into it; shirk the heavy labour, disobey the rules—I will admonish and endeavour to incite you; if in vain, I will flog you; if still in vain, I will at last shoot you—and make God's Earth, and the forlorn-hope in God's Battle, free of you. Understand it I advise you!

Carlyle, *The Latter-Day Pamphlets*, London: 1850, pp. 1-50.

to the principles of freedom and fraternity, as Russian serfdom, Austrian military despotism, and English class legislation. Democracy is an idea, which is still seeking an adequate mode of expression; a soul in want of a body; an ideal, hitherto deemed a chimera—but which is rapidly tending towards a realization in the phenomenal world. One cannot apply any past form of experience, as the measure of a new thought, without getting involved in endless absurdity. The idea predominant in this pamphlet, and which, I think, pervades all Mr Carlyle's works—is that of hero-worship. "*Government, by the best and noblest*"—but however true this idea may be, it is sometimes pushed by him to the extremity of denying the rights of personality—of individual man.

> *The majority have no rights but the one of being governed by the best and noblest of the minority, certainly for public, not for private ends; but by force, by the whip, if need be. Further, the best and noblest are not attainable by consulting the will of the majority, either by means of 'universal ballot-boxing', or otherwise.*[1]

This, I call taking a one-sided view of the case. Masses of men can never be *coerced* into the acknowledgement of truth, or into taking steps towards the realisation of an idea. You must *show them* that a thing is true, and good to be done, then they will follow you joyfully, willingly, as a god-given leader and guide. No man ever governed any country, by the will of its own people, *how expressed* matters not, unless he were the organ chosen by the spirit of the age, the exponent of the Idea which governed that particular epoch, manifesting itself in the whole civilisation of that people. If the governors express the *Idea of their age*, there is no need of coercion, everything goes on smoothly, in obedience to a natural law. Society follows its chiefs as gladly as the Crusaders did Baldwin or Peter the Hermit.[2] But if the governors *stand in direct opposition* to the spirit of their age—i.e., to the thing which the soul of the world, the universal reason incarnate in man, is tending to do at a given historical epoch—society refuses to follow its governors, and we have an epoch of disorganisation and revolution. An epoch where *coercion* is the necessary condition for the existence of these 'sham governors'—who are *not*

---

1. Thomas Carlyle, *Illustrated London News*, 1871.
2. Peter the Hermit (c.1050–1115), a priest of Amiens, and Baldwin (c.1058–1118), son of Eustace II, Count of Boulogne, were leaders of the First Crusade. Baldwin was crowned the King of Jerusalem in 1100.

the exponents of any truth, but the representatives of the ghosts of old, dead, formulas; *not* the legitimate leaders of society, but charlatans and humbugs, who ought to be kicked indefinitely into infinite space—*beyond* creation, if that were practicable.

The present epoch is such a one of disorganisation and revolution. Society is pulling one way, its pretended chiefs another way. I am free to confess that, for me, the most joyful of all spectacles, possible in these times is the one over which Mr Carlyle laments; one which I enjoyed extremely in Vienna, in March 1848, i.e. *"a universal tumbling of impostors and impostures into the street"*.[1] For it just amounts to this, that men are determined to live no longer in lies, but to abolish them at whatever cost. *Ca ira!* And how do men come to perceive that the old social forms are worn out and useless? By the advent of a new Idea. At such an epoch the universal reason has reached so high a degree of development in individual man, that, when the thought, the Fact, of the epoch, is presented to society, it is *seen* to be true. As for the adherents of the old system, they attempt to enforce order by means of coercion, they crucify or shoot men; but the Idea is a subtle thing and eludes their grasp. We may safely predict that the Democratic Idea will survive the butcheries of a Haynau, as it has survived the spears of the Roman legions. For, on all sides, spring up, as if by magic, *"the enemies of order, the Anarchists, Socialists, Chartist vagabonds"*—men, who now, as in the olden time, refuse tribute to Caesar, denounce the Scribes and Pharisees, and preach the gospel to the poor; men who are *"followed by great multitudes, and gladly heard by the common people"*. The new epoch has no lack of soldiers to fight its battles. Mr Carlyle qualifies Red Republicanism—i.e. the Democracy, *which he admits is the Fact of the 19th century,* by the epithet—*"mere inarticulate bellowing"*. This reminds

---

1. Carlyle, *The Latter-Day Pamphlets*, #1, 'The Present Time', p. 12. Within weeks of the overthrow of the French King, Louis Philippe, in February 1848, the citizens of Vienna overthrew the government of Prince Metternich and forced Emperor Ferdinand to concede a parliament and new constitution. But in October, Imperial troops stormed the city and the new Emperor, Franz Joseph, annulled the constitution. In Hungary however, the imperial army was driven out and independence was declared. After Russian troops invaded Hungary and restored Hapsburg rule, the Austrian field marshall, von Haynau, unleashed his own troops on the defeated Hungarian population in an orgy of reprisals.

me of the old saying—"*he that hath ears, let him hear what the Spirit saith to the churches*".[1] Red Republicanism is just about one of the most articulate, plain-speaking voices, in the whole of Universal History. I opine, it is not very difficult to reach the true meaning of this Fact, but we must study it by the light of eighteen centuries of Christianity, or what has hitherto *passed for such*.

Let us see what this frightful bugbear of a *"Democracy, the Fact of the 19th century"* really is. I am aware it is the nightmare and 'old bogy' of all respectable formalists—of all decent money-loving, rate paying, church-going persons, who defer to the opinions of society, and ask of a thing—*"what will people say of it?"* Not, is it *true?* Is it *right?* Persons, in short, who are well affected towards the *"glorious British Constitution"*, and think it cheap at the trifling price of some fifty millions a year. But to another class of people, those unfortunates who have lost all respect for *"hereditary and constituted authority"*—who consider the lawn sleeves of consecrated bishops and the wigs of learned judges, to be so many rags, so much horsehair—diverted from their legitimate and more useful ends—to all such persons, *"Democracy, the Idea of the 19th century"*, is a great and most welcome Fact. This idea has revealed itself at different times, and in different ways. I find it has assumed *four* forms, which, at first sight, are very unlike each other, yet they are only different ways of expressing the same thing, or, to speak strictly, they are the necessary moments in the development, or unfolding, of the idea: and the last of these forms presupposes the foregoing ones—as the fruit presupposes the flower, and that again, the bud. These forms are, the religion taught by the divine Galilean Republican—the reformation of the 16th century—the German philosophy from Immanuel Kant to Hegel, and the Democracy of our own times.

---

1. Revelation 2:17 (King James Bible): "*He that hath an ear, let him hear what the Spirit saith unto the churches; To him that overcometh will I give to eat of the hidden manna, and will give him a white stone, and in the stone a new name written, which no man knoweth saving he that receiveth it.*"

Part two

Tous les peuples sont Freres.
Pierre Dupont[1]

What is the idea which has needed and found so many different modes of expression? It is *Pantheism*. It is the doctrine that the soul and nature, thought and existence, the absolute and the conditioned, the infinite and the finite, *God and man, are identical. Upon this doctrine alone*, rests that holy religion of freedom and love, of the *divinity and brotherhood of man*, in which we, the communists, socialists, and *"republican vagabonds"* of the 19th century, rejoice—as did our precursors, the early oriental converts who did homage to this sublime idea, *"the holy and faithful brethren"*—of whom it is written, that there *"was none among who wanted, for they had all things in common"*.[2] This idea was first promulgated in the form of a dogma, which has always been the case hitherto, with the thought destined to be the vital principle of a particular historical epoch, to be the informing, plastic spirit of a given age—manifesting its character in the whole civilisation of that age, as the character of individual man may be known by his actions; the tree by its fruit. The dogma of which I speak is the incarnation of the Father, of the infinite, the absolute—*"God manifest in the flesh"*. In this form, revealed by Jesus, lies the identity of the divine and human nature, lies pantheism, or the sublime and cheering doctrine of *man's infinity*—as the oak lies folded up in the acorn. *"He that hath seen me hath seen the father"*.[3] *"I am the vine, ye are the branches"*.[4] These and similar expressions have been distorted into every possible form of mythological absurdity—yet their real meaning is clear enough, and shines through the traditional wrappage. It is simply this: the divine nature (or at least a manifestation of it which is found *only in man*) is common to us

---

1. Pierre Dupont (1821–1870) was a celebrated working class songwriter, born in Lyon. In 1850 he was being prosecuted by the French authorities because of his socialist views (condemned to seven years of exile, the sentence was cancelled on appeal). Charles Baudelaire wrote an enthusiastic preface for Dupont's collection, *Chant des Ouvriers (Song of the Workers)* in 1851.
2. Acts 4:32
3. John 14:9
4. John 15:5

all. If we acknowledge and respect the presence of this power in ourselves, we are as much bound to acknowledge and respect its presence in others. *In virtue of our common nature*, we are bound to do to others, as we would they should do to us. This rule is *universally valid*, without distinction of birth, age, rank, sex, country, colour, cultivation, or the like. Wherever you find a human being, you must consider him a brother and treat him as such; doing all for him in case of need, that you would wish done for yourself in a similar case.

Upon the doctrine of man's divinity, rests the distinction between a *person* and a *thing*. It is the reason *why* the most heinous crime I can perpetrate, is invading the personality of my brother man; *using him up* in any way, from murder and slavery downwards. Red Republicanism, or *"Democracy the Fact of the 19th century"—is a protest against this using up of man by man*. It is the endeavour to reduce the golden rule of the Syrian master[1] to practice. Modern democracy is a Christianity manifested in a form adapted to the wants of the present age; it is Christianity divested of its mythological envelope; it is the idea appearing as *pure thought, independent of history and tradition*. In order to arrive at this form, the idea had to pass through the two forms of Protestantism and Philosophy. Protestantism was the re-assertion of the *rights of the personality*.

The right of the individual judgment was placed in opposition to the authority of the church. A limitation to the progress of the human intellect was done away with, man became free of the kingdom of thought, and could henceforward range it at will. This great work had been begun by the Lollards and other heretics of the middle ages, but its accomplishment was reserved for Luther and his contemporaries.[2] They prepared the way for the German philosophy; for that unique and profound investigation into the nature of man—which, conducted by a phalanx of great thinkers, was terminated by Hegel, the last and greatest

---

1. Saul of Tarsus, alias the Apostle Paul.

2. The Lollards were followers of John Wyclif, or 'Wycliffe' (c.1320–1384) a theologian at Balliol College, Oxford, who wanted the Church reformed and its wealth removed. Martin Luther (1483–1546) defied the Catholic Church by nailing his ninety-five theses to the door of the castle church of Wittenburg in 1517. Excommunicated by Pope Leo X, he became the seminal figure of the Protestant Reformation.

of modern philosophers. The result of this investigation was the democratic idea, but as *thought*, not in the inadequate form of a history or saga. As Hegel expresses it, *"Freedom is a necessary element in the conception, man"*. The German thinkers, from Kant to Hegel, were the apostles and pioneers of the democratic movement, at present shaking society to its foundation, throughout the German empire. The next step in the history of this idea, will be its practical realization, i.e., the reconstruction of society in accordance with the democratic idea. Is it for a moment to be supposed that this idea—having, despite all opposition, passed through so many phases, or moments, of its development—will stop short of the next and final one? Certainly not. Our opponents say to us—*"You are a small contemptible faction of proletarians, led by a few designing demagogues, and yet you pretend to change the face of the civilised world! You set yourselves in opposition to us; to the governments of Europe, with their standing armies; to the aristocracy, with its vast territorial possessions and its feudal privileges; to the state churches, with their immense wealth; and to the bourgeoisie, with its competitive system, its sordid, grasping, avaricious spirit, so completely opposed to all generous impulses, all noble aspirations!"* We answer, *"Yes, O wise men (of Gotham)![1] We are not only so mad as to do this very thing, but we go the insane length of looking calmly forward to the time when you and your system of atrocious lies will be swept into outer darkness, into the domain of the father of lies—whereto in fact, you properly belong"*. All experience is against us, it is said. I think one of the most astonishing 'experiences' in the history of humanity, was the appearance of the democratic idea in the person of a poor despised Jewish proletarian, the Galilean carpenter's son, who worked—probably at his father's trade—till he was thirty years of age, and then began to teach this idea, wrapped in parables and figures—to other working-men; chiefly fishermen, it is said, who listened to him while they mended their nets, or cast them into the lake of Gennesaret. What matter, though, in order to elabo-

---

1. According to legend, the people of Gotham, Nottinghamshire refused to allow a public highway through their village. When King John planned to visit on a hunting trip, and sent his royal messengers to inspect accessibility, they found all the villagers engaged in absurd tasks, such as rolling a cheese down a hill and trying to drown an eel in a pond. After the royal visit was called off, the villagers—who seem to have been only pretending to be rustic imbeciles—commented, *"we ween there are more fools pass through Gotham than remain in it"*.

rate the democratic idea, the soul has required eighteen centuries of labour, and agony, and bloody sweat—continued through a never-failing succession of organs—from that agony, in Gethsemane, of its first organ for the expression of the idea that God and man are one? The anticipation of this ultimate fact has now become reality; and *faith* has been transfigured into *knowledge*. Men die, but thought, the absolute—exists forever. Outward phenomena, its manifestations, its modes of expression—are evanescent. Yet never has there been a lack of organs for the soul, from that thorn-crowned martyr on Calvary, and his early disciples, scourged, tortured, torn in pieces by the wild beasts of the Roman amphitheatres, branded as the *"enemies of order and the human race"*—down to the noble martyrs, who, in our days, have joined the sacred band, the *"great cloud of witnesses"*,[1] for the divine idea of love and freedom, first taught by our elder brother, the crucified Nazarean proletarian.[2]

The blood of our martyrs saturates the soil of Europe; they languish in dungeons; they pine in exile; they have joyfully sacrificed their holiest affections on the altar of liberty; they have often endured *worse than crucifixion*, in seeing their defenceless wives and daughters given up to the brutality of a savage and

---

1. Hebrews 12:1

2. From Marx's 'Contribution to the Critique of Hegel's Philosophy of Right: Introduction (1844): *"Clearly the weapon of criticism cannot replace the criticism of weapons, and material force must be overthrown by material force; but theory also becomes a material force as soon as it has gripped the masses. Theory is capable of gripping the masses when it demonstrates* ad hominem, *and it demonstrates* ad hominem *as soon as it becomes radical. To be radical is to grasp things by the root. But, for man, the root is man himself. Clear proof of the radicalism of German theory and its practical energy is the fact that it takes as its point of departure a decisive and positive transcendence of religion. The criticism of religion ends with the doctrine that* man is the supreme being for man, *and thus with the* categorical imperative to overthrow all conditions *in which man is a debased, enslaved, neglected and contemptible being... Just as philosophy finds its material weapons in the proletariat, so the proletariat finds its intellectual weapons in philosophy... The emancipation of the German is the emancipation of man. The head of this emancipation is philosophy, its heart the proletariat. Philosophy cannot realize itself without the transcendence* [Aufhebung] *of the proletariat, and the proletariat cannot transcend itself without the realization* [Verwirklichung] *of philosophy."* Marx, *Early Writings*, London, 1975, p. 251-57.

licentious soldiery.[1] Yet we do not weep for the sufferings of our beloved brothers. We rejoice for these heroes of humanity, *"who have fought the good fight, and endured to the end"*. And if the age in which the democratic idea first appeared, in a mythical and inadequate form, has been called miraculous and divine—what shall be said of the present age, which has seen the manifestation of this idea in the form of pure thought, divested of the opaque element of empiricism, independent of all tradition, of all Sagas? *"The kingdom of God is like a grain of mustard seed, which, when it is sown, is less than all the seeds that are in the ground. But when it is sown, it shooteth up, and becometh the greatest of all herbs, and spreadeth out great branches so that the fowls of their air can lodge under its shadow".*[2] It is the tree of life and of liberty, *"whose leaves are for the healing of the nations"*,[3] under whose shadow, not only the fowls of the air, but the weary and heavy laden human soul may lodge and find rest. But its shade will never gladden us, my proletarian brothers! There is no rest for the present generation. Are we foolish enough to expect an El Dorado—a paradise created by *"Acts of a reformed parliament"*—(a *fool's paradise*, in such a case, I think) lying open to us? That we have nothing to do, but to march in and take possession? Alas! we know that the battle between the old and new epochs—between falsehood and truth, selfishness and love, despotism and freedom—will be *long, bloody, and terrible*. Through revolutions which have already begun, through fearful social convulsions, through wars and calamities, will the children of light triumph—after long years, it may be—over the powers of darkness. The Greek myth sets forth, that Hercules conquered the kingdom of heaven by his *valour*, only *after* a long series of labours and sufferings, and at the last—a painful death—was he admitted among the gods, and united to Hebe, the personification of immortal youth and joy. This is as true *now* as it was in the days of Homer—or earlier—when all men devoutly believed it. We must *work*, then, before we can enter *our heaven*.[4]

---

1. See below, Helen Macfarlane's essay on Julius Jacob von Haynau's atrocities in Hungary, 'The Morning Post and the Woman Flogger'.
2. Mark 4:32
3. Revelation 22:2
4. See also, *"You gotta wade through miles of shit/To get to paradise"* Geronimo Black 'Trail of Tears', *Welcome Back*, Helios, 1980: *"the*

I apprehend, the most pressing work required from the present pioneers of the new epoch is the *work of destruction*. For a new form of society can rise only upon the ruins of the old one. Before the new heaven and the new earth can be created, the old heaven and the old earth must be *"rolled up like a scroll"*,[1] and be altogether abolished. We must not hesitate about pulling down the old rotten framework of society, even though, like the brave Hebrew of old, we ourselves should be slain with the Philistines— buried in the ruins of this old temple of Dagon, which reeks with the blood of human victims, and is filled to overflowing with all manner of abominations and wickedness.[2] We demand the total demolition of the present system of things, because the social arrangements now obtaining in Europe, are, *without exception*, so radically bad that the democratic idea finds in them obstacles only in the way of its realization. It was asked of old, *"What fellowship is there between Christ and Belial?"*[3] In our modern way of expressing the same thing, I ask, what correspondence is there between the democratic idea and social forms expressing a much lower grade of intellectual development—social arrangements based on principles belonging to antique times, when this idea was wholly unknown? Upon what principle of a *hitherto unknown logic*, will you reconcile such diametrically opposite things, as the idea of fraternity—and our pagan hierarchy of state priests, our laws founded upon Roman jurisprudence, our cast of hereditary legislators, and our selfish competitive system?

Part three

I have said that Red Republicanism, or the democracy which is the *"Fact of the 19th century"*, is not *"mere inarticulate bellowing"*. We democrats know extremely well *why* we demand the aboli-

---

transcendence of self-estrangement follows the same course of self-estrangement", Marx, MECW, Vol. 4, p. 281.

1. Revelation 6:14: *"And the heaven departed as a scroll when it is rolled together; and every mountain and island were moved out of their places."*

2. Dagon, the deity of the Philistines, was a half-man, half-fish creature. When Samson was captured by the Philistines, he sacrificed himself by bringing down the pillars of the Temple of Dagon with his bare arms (Judges 16:30).

3. 2 Corinthians 6:15

tion of existing social forms. It is because they are altogether opposed to the democratic, or Christian idea. They do not express this idea at all. They are fragments of an earlier world, a confused jumble of Jewish, Teutonic, and Roman laws, usages, and superstitions; in which the idea of our epoch has found a very narrow and uncomfortable habitation. In these old ruins it has—for many centuries—been *"cribbed, cabined, and confined"*,[1] till it has grown strong enough now to break through the walls of its dungeons. Society, as at present constituted, throughout the civilised world—*in America as well as in Europe*—does *not* express the Christian idea of equality and fraternity, but the totally opposite pagan principle of inequality an selfishness. In the antique world, the position of a man was determined by the accident of birth. As a citizen of Athens, or of Rome, he was free. But these Athenian and Roman citizens denied the same rights to men belonging to all other nations, whom they contemptuously styled barbarians. They enslaved these other men, or used them up as chattels—in a variety of ways, according as it was found profitable or convenient; precisely as the *"free and enlightened citizens of America"* do coloured men at the present day. This conduct was excusable enough in the nations of antiquity. The wisest among them could, in fact, act in no other way. *For the true nature of man was not then understood.* Neither in the religion, nor in the philosophy, of the ancient world, do we find the *divinity of human nature* expressed. Among all the rich variety of forms assumed by the antique civilisation, there is not one which expresses this fundamental idea of Christianity or democracy, either in a mythical or speculative form. The ancient philosophers left many questions untouched which now occupy a great space in the territory of speculation. For example:

> *the inquiries into the faculty of cognition, into the opposition of subjectivity and objectivity, were unknown in Plato's time. The absolute independence of the personality, its existence for and through itself, were quite unknown to Plato. Man had not then returned—so to speak—into himself, had not thoroughly inves-*

---

1. Shakespeare, *Macbeth* 13: Act 3 scene 4.

    Macbeth: *Then comes my fit again: I had else been perfect; Whole as the marble, founded as the rock, As broad and general as the casing air: But now I am cabined, cribbed, confined, bound in, To saucy doubts and fears. But Banquo's safe?*

tigated his own nature. This individual subject was indeed independent, free—but was conscious of this only as an isolated fact. The Athenian, the Roman, knew he was free. But that man, *as such, is free—as a human being, is born free—was unknown alike to Plato and to Aristotle, to Cicero and to the Roman jurists, although this conception alone is the source of all jurisprudence. In Christianity we find, for the first time, the individual personal soul depicted as possessing an infinite, absolute value. God wills the salvation of all men. In this religion we find the doctrine that the whole human race is equal in the sight of God, redeemed from bondage, and introduced into a state of Christian freedom by Jesus. These modes of representation make freedom independent of rank, birth, cultivation, and the like; and the progress which has been made by this means is immense. Yet this mode of viewing the matter is somewhat different from the fact that freedom is an indispensable element in the conception— man. The undefined feeling of this fact has worked for centuries in the dark; the instinct of freedom has produced the most terrible revolutions, but the* idea *of the innate freedom of man—this* knowledge *of his own nature—is not old.*[1]

These two modes of viewing the matter are the necessary *complements of each other*. The one mode is imaginative, the other intellectual; the one is religious, the other philosophical. The first mode presents the democratic idea in the form of a myth; the second presents it in the more appropriate and developed form of a conception—as a product of pure reason. But they both belong to the modern world. In the whole civilisation of the human race, there is not a trace of the democratic idea to be found, until the appearance of the Nazarean. This being the case, might we not reasonably expect that the forms assumed by modern civilisation would be *essentially different* from those assumed by the antique

---

1. J.H. Muirhead, in his 1928 essay, 'How Hegel Came to England', wrongly claims, "*Up to the middle of the [eighteen] fifties it may be said that no intelligible word had been spoken by British writers as to the place and significance of Hegel's work*" (See Peter Nicholson, Review of P Robbins, 'The British Hegelians 1875-1925', *Bulletin of the Hegel Society of Great Britain* No.3, 1983). All commentators on the nineteenth-century 'British Hegelians', have missed Macfarlane's 'first' as a translator of, and commentator on, Hegel's philosophical writings (George Henry Lewes translated some passages of Hegel in an essay entitled 'Hegel's Aesthetics', in the *British and Foreign Review* #13, 1842).

culture? Vain expectation! *"The centuries are conspirators against the sanity and majesty of the soul"*, says an American writer.[1] We are haunted by the ghosts of old dead nations and cultures, and whenever we say, *"let us have done with the past, there is nothing in it any longer sacred for us, we find no form in it for our idea"*; we are beset by the party of the past, who terrify a weak-minded public by the stereotype cry, *"The Church is in danger, the landed—the manufacturing—interest, is in danger! Every one who interferes with the system by which we thrive, is a demagogue, a Chartist vagabond, who wishes to unsettle society! Your idea? Bah! It has never yet been!"* Sometimes the devil can speak truth. It is a God's truth, my proletarian brothers, that our idea has never yet been. No Jewish theocracy, or Gothic feudality or Roman imperialism, will fit this idea. It is certainly not expressed in our state church, with her secular head and her pagan hierarchy of bishops—like the flamens of Jupiter with Caesar as Pontifex Maximus; not in her Jewish system of tithes, fasts, and superstitious sabbath observances; her white-robed priests, chaunting litanies, and repeating endless prayers—a set of men specially *"dedicated to the service of the altar"*, like the Levites of old. Let us look a little at the working of *this* social form. The work set aside for the priests of the state church is the christianising of the English people. For performing the same, these priests receive from ten to twelve millions sterling a year of national property. I call *church* property *national* property, because government, supposed (by the John Doe and Richard Roe fiction of *"a glorious British constitution"*) to represent the British people, having once taken this property from a sect of religionists and bestowed it upon another sect, *could change its destination a second time*, if needful. Queen Elizabeth—in the main a woman of sound sense—had a clear perception of the legal tenure of church property, when she told a refractory bishop, *"God's death! I that frocked you will unfrock you!"*[2] By Christianising a nation, I understand instructing all the persons composing it in the principles of justice and charity, inculcated as the *beginning*

---

1. The 'American writer' is Ralph Waldo Emerson: *"Is the acorn better than the oak which is its fullness and completion? Is the parent better than the child into whom he has cast his ripened being? Whence, then, this worship of the past? The centuries are conspirators against the sanity and authority of the soul."* Ralph Waldo Emerson, 'Self-Reliance', *Essays: New Series*, 1841.
2. The refractory bishop was Sir Richard Cox, who was elected Bishop of Norwich in 1559, but 'demoted' by the queen to the bishopric of Ely.

and end of his religion, by the founder of Christianity. The machinery requisite for the purpose exists. The whole of England is covered with a network of churches and chapels, where, on appointed days, the state priests read prayers and discourse on theological dogmas, to well-fed, well-dressed persons, chiefly of the middle and higher classes. But *"to the poor the gospel is (not) preached"*; and all allusion to the vicious and anti-Christian constitution of modern society on the principle of selfishness, with its two great ramifications of despotism and mammon-worship— is avoided as if the subject were red-hot iron. The state priests are far behind the idea of the age, and yet they pretend to guide society! Human intelligence has now expanded beyond the limits of mediæval church symbols. I do not find that these pretended preachers of the precepts of Jesus are even commonly honest men, who refuse to take the wages when they *cannot* do the work. No English archbishop—head of the church—or overseer of moral training—has ever gone to the English government, and said:

> *Gentlemen, you pay us an enormous sum of money yearly for christianising the English people, but you give us this work* clogged with impossible conditions. *Your social arrangements are such, that thousands upon thousands of persons are forever condemned to live in a horrible state of misery, of actual starvation, and are inevitably driven—by the powerful instinct of self-preservation, by the cravings of hunger—to the* perpetual commission of abominable vices, *in order to keep soul and body yet a little while longer together. We read aloud the gospel,* "suffer little children to come unto me and forbid them not, for of such is the kingdom of God".[1] *The practical commentary on this text, is the fact—that children of ten and twelve years of age find no alternative between* dying of hunger and living by prostitution. *As long as the* causes *which produce this lamentable state of things continue to work, our hands are tied. Organise labour. Make it, first of all,* possible for your subjects to live, then *you may ask us to teach them to* live virtuously.

The state priests pocket all the wages they can get, cry out for more, and leave the work to take care of itself. Even when a middle-class liberal comes forward, with a modest plan for patching and mending the old rotten system a little—like Mr Fox with his

---

1. Matthew 19:14

Education Bill[1]—these clerical hypocrites raise a shriek of woe as if heaven and earth were falling to pieces! Is the case any better with the state church in Scotland, or dissenters generally? I think not. They have not so much wealth as the English Church; certain striking deviations from the Christian principle of equality and fraternity are not so rife in these churches; but in reality they are as pagan as the church of Rome, or of England. Does any sect now extant acknowledge the doctrine of man's infinity? That in Christianity there is no *limitation whatever*, except the moral imperative; that idea of duty towards others which necessarily arises out of the very constitution of the human soul? *"If ye love one another, ye are my disciples"*.[2] Except in violation of this law of fraternity, I may act and think in any manner I choose; I may range the kingdoms of spirit and matter at will, with none to make me afraid. What a noble idea is this theoretical and practical freedom of man, his *infinite possibilities*—which lies at the bottom of the Christian myths and sagas, and has now assumed the form of Democracy! A noble idea, but—good heavens! what a miserable, contemptible reality.

All sects hedge me in with limitations. I cannot move a step in any direction without running against some creed, or catechism, or formula, which rises up like a wall between the unhappy sectarians and the rest of the universe; beyond which it is forbidden to look on pain of damnation, or worse. No sect has ever yet raised its voice against the iniquitous inequality obtaining between the different ranks of society, whereby the accident of birth alone determines whether a human being shall have the culture necessary to develop his moral and intellectual powers—the culture without which he cannot obtain dominion over his animal wants and appetites, but must remain—like a beast—under the sway of instinct. No sect, whether established or dissenting, has ever protested against the social arrangements, in virtue of which the existence of such human brutes as that poor boy lately discovered in the diocese of the Bishop of London, is permitted—I almost said—no—but encouraged, and indeed made inevitable. Yet such a state of society is as much opposed to the Christian

---

1. William Johnson Fox (1786–1864), MP for Oldham, was a Unitarian preacher at South Place Chapel, later known as the South Place Ethical Society (at Conway Hall, London). His reforming Education Bill of 1850 failed to get passed in Parliament.

2. John 13:35

idea of universal fraternity as the Hindoo institution of caste. With us the poor are the Chandalas, the unclean outcasts of society, which ignores their very existence, unless it be to punish them for crimes, the commission of which society ought to have prevented by providing *all* its members—first, with the means of comfortable subsistence; and secondly, with the means of moral and intellectual cultivation. Hypocritical teachers of Paganism in the guise of Christianity! Have done with this preaching and prating about things which you scarcely even *profess*, and undoubtedly do not *practice*.

You talk of the *"visible church of Christ"*, but you do all in your power to make it an extremely invisible church. Some of you talk much about certain persons whom you call the *"Fathers of the Church"*, but if these venerable fathers could become cognisant of your proceedings, they certainly would refuse to acknowledge *you* for sons. For it impossible to find any two things more opposed than the doctrines concerning justice and brotherly love taught by the 'Fathers', and the system pursued by you. If these worthy men were to rise from the dead, they would be found in *our ranks*; they would be Democrats, Demagogues, Socialists, Communists, Jacobins, Enemies of Order, of society, and of *you*.

St. Ambrose says, in express terms, that *"property is usurpation"*. St. Gregory the Great[1] regards landed proprietors as so many assassins:

> *Let them know that the earth, from which they were created, is the common property of all men; and that, therefore, the fruits of the earth belong indiscriminately to All. Those who make private property of the gift of God, pretend in vain to be innocent! For, in thus retaining the subsistence of the poor, they are the Murderers of those who die every day for want of it.*

What an incendiary vagabond is this 'Venerable Father!' St. John, called from his eloquence, Chrysostomus, or Goldenmouth, says:

> *Behold the idea we ought to have concerning rich and avaricious men. They are robbers who beset highways, strip travellers, and then hoard up the property of others, in the houses which are their dens.*

St. Augustine says on the subject of inheritance;

---

1. Pope Gregory I (c.540–604).

> *Beware of making parental affection a pretext for the augmentation of your possessions—I keep my wealth for my children—vain excuse! Your father kept it for you, you keep it for your children, and they will keep it for theirs, and so on. But in this way no one would observe the law of God!*

St. Basil the great, in his *Treatise di Avarit*. 21, p. 328, Paris ed. 1638, asks;

> *Who is the robber? It is he who appropriates to himself the things which belong to All. Art thou not a robber, thou who takest for thyself the goods thou has received from God for the purpose of distributing them to others? If he who steals a garment be called a robber, ought not the possessor of garments, who refrains from clothing the naked, to be called by the same name? The bread thou hast stored belongs to him who is hungry; the garment thou keepest in reserve belongs to him who is naked; the sandals thou hast lying by belong to him who goes barefoot; and the money thou hast hoarded—as if buried in the earth—belongs to him who has none.*

Louis Blanc is a very tame and moderate person, I think, compared with the Communists I have just quoted.[1] How comes it that *you, soi-disant* preachers of the gospel of Christ, never take these or similar extracts from the *"Fathers of the Christian church"*, as texts for your homilies? I have frequently heard you quote from St. Augustine on *predestination and grace*, but you preserve a mysterious silence regarding St. Augustine *on property*. It is because you neither teach the Christian idea, nor do you live in it; because you are a set of pitiable impostors. You do not even *make a profession* of those precepts of Fraternity taught by the Nazarean, and said *by him* to contain the true spirit of his religion. You wisely keep silence on such points, else—out of your own lying mouths—would you be convicted. You leave an immense and ever-increasing mass of destitution and ignorance, and crime, lying untouched at your own doors; you enter no protest against the system of civilisation—*rotten to its very core*—which has produced, and which fosters, this hideous state of things; but you fly to the

---

1. Louis Blanc (1811–1882) was a leading socialist member of the French provisional government established in February 1848. Following the counter-revolution of the June Days he was driven into exile and lived in London.

uttermost parts of the earth—to China or Timbuktu—in search of objects for the exercise of your boundless and overflowing Christian charity; and some among you have been found impudent enough to raise objections when others have proposed doing somewhat to enlighten the ignorance of which I speak. Pah! one's very soul is sickened by such atrocious humbug. Is the democratic idea expressed with greater fidelity in any other phases of the civilisation now extant? In class legislation? In the exorbitant price of Law, whereby what is called Justice is placed beyond the reach of any save the Rich? In the Knowledge Tax?[1] In the scanty measure of sectarian education dealt out to us by priests? In our system of *indirect* taxation, whereby the public burdens fall *heaviest* on the class which is *least able* to support them? In the law of primogeniture, whereby one member of a family is 'made a gentleman', and the rest left beggars, to be kept by the producers— as state priests, bureaucrats, soldiers, pensioners—whose name is legion? In a caste of hereditary legislators? In the position of women, who are regarded by the law not as *persons* but as *things*, and placed in the same category as children and the insane?

Society, as at present constituted, is directly opposed to the democratic idea; and must, therefore, be remodelled. To ask, my proletarian brothers, is one thing, but to *get* is another thing— a hopeless thing, I should say, from a government which does nothing unless compelled by the pressure from without, and which—instead of being its proper place—at the head of advancing society, disgracefully lags in the rear. One is disgusted by the impudent state jugglery called *"a change of ministry"*, (yet without the least change in the principles of administration) whereby one set of charlatans succeed another set *ad infinitum*—Tories, Conservatives, Whigs—but the one set of state quacks just as little as the other set, never do anything to better the sad condition of the suffering masses. An unprecedented fact lately existed in the shape of a Whig surplus, but—as to the Knowledge Tax, why a Whig chancellor could not *"see any reason for its priority"* in this matter of relief—

> ... *and in fact, my dear fellows!* our *position as Whig officials is not affected by the consideration whether* you *are stinted or not in the means of satisfying the primary wants of humanity,*

---

1. The 'Knowledge Tax' was the Newspaper Stamp Duty, which was finally abolished in 1855.

> stinted in food for the body and soul. You 'men in blouses' cannot understand our reasons exactly—but we beg to observe that her majesty's ministers are determined to preserve the peace of the manufacturing districts, and that model prisons for Chartist vagabonds exist, where skilly[1] is made on admirable principles.

To me a Whig is a still more noxious animal than a Tory. So-called 'Liberals' are fast becoming a nuisance. I recognise only two parties in the political world. These are Democrats and Aristocrats; the friends and the enemies of the people. Between these parties there can be no compromise, it is war to the knife between them. No measure of a surface and partial character—the 'Reforms', for instance, proposed by your *respectable* middle class little charter professors of 'liberal' humbug—will ever satisfy the claims of the Democratic idea. Aristocracy—that insane delusion whereby one part of society arrogates to itself so immense a superiority over another part, as to deny the primary rights of humanity to this last—has assumed many forms. Of these, the basest is bourgeois-aristocracy, for it is founded upon mammon-worship. A 'grace of God' madman, like Charles the Tenth, may possibly be a gentleman; but a greengrocer, stockbrokering Louis Philippe, with a clientèle of *"opulent shopkeepers and respectable manufacturers"*, is the *acme* of all that is sordid and contemptible.[2] In what a ridiculous position have the bourgeoisie of this country lately placed themselves! In that trumpery 'Conference' held last month by the leaders of the middle class reformers, the selfish, sectarian nature of the middle class movement came out in glaring colours. These 'free-trade and big loaf' gentry have been shamefully beaten on every measure they have introduced into *"the hospital of Incurables"* this session—yet they will do anything rather than coalesce with the proletarians—they have grievously wronged the working men of England, *therefore they fear Universal Suffrage*. My proletarian brothers, we have had too severe lessons as to the hypocritical nature of bourgeois friendship—viz.: the

---

1. Skilly was a thin gruel served up in prisons.
2. The Bourbon King, Charles X (1757–1836), ruled France from 1824 until 1830, when he was overthrown and replaced by the 'Bourgeois Monarch' Louis Philippe (1773–1850)—who was himself deposed by the 1848 Revolution.

Reform Bill and the League.[1] Let us tell these middle class monkeys, "*if you want roasted chestnuts, use your own paws to take them out of the fire. We refuse to be made catspaws of any longer for your advantage*". Without the proletarians to back him, how can Mr Cobden get up the "*storm of agitation*" he promised us? "*superior pyrotechny this evening!!*"—only the fireworks are not forthcoming![2] Let us stand aloof and leave the middle class leaders to their own resources yet awhile. I have heard that 'Manchester men' are famous hands at a bargain. Messrs. Cobden and Bright will need all their commercial ability when they are obliged, as they will be at no distant time, to come to terms with the leaders of the despised and trampled-on proletarians. Let us do all in our power, my Socialist-democratic brothers, to hasten the advent of this time by means of an ever-increasing, ever-spreading agitation on the subject of our principles. Let us establish a veritable democratic propaganda. Let us listen to the voice of our martyred Galilean brother speaking words of hope and consolation to us across bygone centuries, and through the records of vanished nations, "*a little leaven leaveneth the whole lump*".[3] Was this true in the time of *Roman* despots only, or is it true now? Let us to the work! If we use the means *without wavering, without faint-heartedness*, we shall certainly obtain this end. Our end is the Organisation of Labour and the final establishment of a pure Democracy; our means, the complete destruction of the Past through a critique of pure Reason. The organisation of labour, upon the associative principle, is our aim, because we will make it possible for the toiling millions of England to live in a state more befitting hu-

---

1. The 'League' was the Anti-Corn Law League, founded in 1838, and led by Richard Cobden (1804–1865) and John Bright (1811–1889). The 'Leaguers' saw the main obstacle to Parliamentary Reform as the landlord class, whose political dominance they sought to break by the repeal of the protectionist Corn Laws. The Corn Laws were repealed by Sir Robert Peel's Conservatives in 1846, but this did not lead to the land of cheap bread and plenty-for-all promised by the free trader .
2. Ralph Waldo Emerson, in a essay on Shakespeare, contrasts the poetic attitude to natural phenomena, such as the stars, with the cheap commercialism of municipal fireworks displays advertised as "*superior pyrotechny this evening*". "*Are the agents of nature, and the power to understand them, worth no more than a street serenade or the breath of a cigar?*" he asks. (*Prose Works of Ralph Waldo Emerson*, Boston: 1870).
3. Galatians 5:9

man beings than a continual hopeless alternation of exhausting toil and starving, wretched idleness. The total destruction of the Past is our means, because existing social forms leave no room for the evolution of the Democratic Idea. Up, then, and be doing! *"To the self-helping mortal the blessed immortals are swift"*, said the Persian Zoroaster.[1] We Socialist-democrats are the soldiers of a holy cause; we are the exponents of a sublime idea; we are the apostles of the sacred religion of universal humanity. We have sworn by the God who *"made of one blood all nations of the Earth"*,[2] that we will not pause till we have finished the great work—begun by the Nazarean—of man's redemption from the social miseries which destroy body and soul. We will not pause till we have freed our own beloved country from the aristocratic despotism under which it groans; not until the rose, the shamrock, and the thistle, be woven into one wreath for the altar of Liberty; not until Saxon and Celt—forgetting their senseless feuds and animosities—rally round the *Red Banner* to the battle-cry of the new epoch, *Vive la Republique, Democratique et Sociale!*

---

1. Ralph Waldo Emerson writes in *Self-reliance, and Other Essays*, p. 33: *"Welcome evermore to gods and men is the self-helping man. For him all doors are flung wide: him all tongues greet, all honors crown, all eyes follow with desire. Our love goes out to him and embraces him, because he did not need it. We solicitously and apologetically caress and celebrate him, because he held on his way and scorned our disapprobation. The gods love him because men hated him. 'To the persevering mortal,' said Zoroaster, 'the blessed Immortals are swift.'"*
2. Acts 17:26

Intrigues of the Middle Class 'Reformers'

Democratic Review, July 1850

Someone, I forget who, once said, *"Save me from my friends, I can defend myself against my enemies"*.[1] That is, from my pretended friends. We, my Proletarian brothers, have cause enough at present, to join in this sensible aspiration. For our pretended friends, the respectable sham-reformers of the Parliamentary and Financial dodge, the leaders of the English Bourgeois movement, have lately come out in their true character, viz., as selfish humbugs. As a set of hypocrites, who, under the mask of friendship for the people, try to take advantage of the generous confidence, erewhile placed (foolishly enough) in them by the latter. I should have expected, however, that practical men of business, belonging to the sharp 'Manchester School', would have managed their dirty underhand intrigues in a less clumsy way. What a blunder, to employ a creature like Clark in so delicate a mission as that of adroitly betraying his former friends![2] A

---

1. The quotation is attributed to Marshal General of France, Claude de Villars (1653–1734), when taking leave of King Louis XIV.
2. Thomas Clark (c.1821-56) was manager of Feargus O'Connor's Land Plan, a scheme to resettle factory workers in smallholding agricultural communities. The scheme, which began in 1845, managed to establish several settlements by lottery of its 70,000 shareholders. George Julian Harney, however, believed that attempting to fight capitalism by establishing peasant smallholdings was reactionary. By 1850, Land Plan was collapsing under the weight of financial mismanagement,

matter requiring the utmost nicety of diplomatic handling! Two guineas a week, besides funds for the establishment of the National Charter League, entirely thrown away! What a distressing fact for the contemplation of a Council of *Financial* Reformers! Where was the economical Joseph Hume during all this? Truly, if these financial gentlemen can show no better title to become Reformers for the National expenditure, than the bad management of their own funds, I think their pretensions are poor enough. English men of business? Why, a French ordermonger, or an Austrian police-clerk, would have done the job in a business-like way, and not made a mess of it, like these bourgeois bunglers and their clumsy tool, Mr Clark, the Chartist renegade. Look you, my Proletarian brothers, had the middle classes not found you so sublimely naif, so foolishly generous, so easily gulled, during the Reform Bill agitation—their leaders would not now have dared to insult your judgment, and tempt your patience, by so barefaced, so impudent, so villainous a trick. What! on the one hand they pretend to be the People's friends—they protest, before God and man, that all their measures are for the benefit of the producers; and on the other hand, they clandestinely attempt to create dissension in the Proletarian Camp; they employ hired traitors and apostates, to blacken the characters of the staunchest and best among the Proletarian leaders; to set them together by the ears, if possible; to divide the Democratic interest into contending sections, so that the attention of the Proletarians might be diverted from the question of questions—a Remedy for the Social miseries under which they suffer.

All this meanness was perpetrated by 'honourable gentlemen', in order that the middle class harpies might continue to prey upon the Proletarians—that bourgeois profit-mongers might use them up in any way that was found convenient—from eighteen hours a day of work at unhealthy trades for a minimum of wages, to monster meetings in Free Trade Halls, for the purpose of applauding the 'thoroughly liberal' clap-trap speeches of Mr John Bright. I am free to confess, that I feel a sort of astonishment at

---

corruption and hostile parliamentary scrutiny. O'Connor's efforts to form and an alliance with radical Liberals, to campaign for the Six-Point People's Charter 'by installments' were spearheaded by Clark. Clark and his supporters in Manchester tried to form a breakaway "National Charter League" which would remove the 'stigma of Redism' from the movement.

Feargus O'Connor, owner of the Northern Star

the cool impertinence of these men. They scarcely take the trouble of throwing a veil over their base manœvres. They seem to think any kind of story will do for the working men. They wholly forget the fact, that *book learning* and *intelligence* are by no means synonymous terms. *"Much learning does not teach a man Reason"*, says Heraclitus,[1] a greater thinker, perhaps, than Malthus—that Apostle and lawgiver of the Manchester school.[2]

Messrs. Cobden and Bright, always remind me of that ridiculous couple, Don Quixote and Sancho Panza. There is a mental hardness and dryness about the one, comparable to nothing in the universe, save the physique of the skinny, lanthorn-jawed Don; and about the other—an obtuse, bull-headed dogmatism, a happy self-complacency, very like Sancho in Barataria, laying down the law about everything and everybody, though unable to see one inch, in any direction, beyond the tip of his own snub-nose. Pity these financial gentlemen had not shared honest Sancho's predilection for the homely wisdom of proverbs. There is one, very applicable to them, which says—*"Show me your companions, and I will tell you what you are"*.

Sir Joshua Walmsley has gained no credit from engaging in a mean, treacherous intrigue for the purpose of breaking up the Chartist movement—a job so dirty, that he was obliged to have such associates therein as Clark and Co.; men whose only weapons were the coarsest slander, the foulest abuse, the grossest personalities. But the very virulence of their attacks on the popular leaders defeated its own end. Did Sir Joshua think that the working men of *"practical, intelligent England"*, were such egregious donkeys as to place confidence in a man whose chief occupation seemed to be abusing the order from which he sprung, the Proletarians, whose hired servant he was, by whose hard money he had been supported; did he suppose that the bitter hatred displayed by Clark in the unmanly, contemptible calumnics he uttered concerning Julian Harney, and others, would be passports to the favour of the people—to whose cause these staunch and consistent Democrats had devoted their whole lives? Bah! Let me advise these financial and commercial gentlemen, the next time they *"do a little"* in *Machiavellism*, to study the adaptation of *means* to *ends*, else they will bring their goods to a bad market. The in-

---

1. Heraclitus of Ephesus (c.535–475 BCE): *"Learning many things does not teach understanding. Else it would have taught Hesiod and Pythagoras, as well as Xenophanes and Hecataeus"*.
2. Most of the Manchester Liberals adhered to the argument of the Reverend Thomas Malthus (1766–1834) that 'pauperism' was simply a product of population growth.

Intrigues of the Middle Class 'Reformers' 27

famous Cæsar Borgia,[1] a pupil of Machiavel,[2] was the prince of the intriguers; a base, treacherous, contemptible rascal—whose name is a bye-word for systematic deceit—but in one particular Borgia did not resemble Sir Joshua Walmsley, for the wily Italian was a man of vigorous intellect, *and knew how to choose his instruments*. It is singular, of what very dirty, disreputable tricks your 'highly respectable' people will sometimes be guilty!

The discovery of these middle class intrigues ought to be matter of rejoicing to every true Democrat. It teaches us a lesson of vital importance. A lesson, my Proletarian brothers, which I would incessantly and unweariedly inculcate—day and night upon you, were that possible. It is this: *put not your faith in middle class money lords, in bourgeois profit-mongers*, even though they wear the mask of liberalism and pretend to be the people's friends. They are the enemies of the veritable people—the producers. *Worse enemies* than Kings, or State Priests, or the landed, hereditary Aristocracy. Look at France for a proof of this assertion. There, monarchy, feudality, and the state church, have been swept away by the revolutionary whirlwind, but the domination of the middle classes yet exists as a system of bourgeois terrorism—of odious, sanguinary despotism—to which it would be difficult to find a match in the history of any civilised nation. Truly has it been said by the Editor of the *Democratic Review*[3]— *"if the landlords scourged us with whips, the money-lords would scourge us with scorpions"*. Notwithstanding all this, notwithstanding their open hostility to the Ten Hours Bill; even to the Parliamentary redtape twaddle of *"An enquiry into the state of the cotton-lords and their Reforming Clique, will at the end of the present session, make a tour through the manufacturing districts, for the purpose of gaining proselytes,*

---

1. Cesare Borgia (1475–1507), bastard son of Pope Alexander VI, was Duke of Valentinois, condottiero, cardinal, assassin, and syphilitic womaniser. By 1502, he had managed to conquer most of Italy, but fell from grace after Julius II became Pope in 1503. After going into exile, he became a military commander in Spain for King John III of Navarre, but was killed in a skirmish with rebel forces.
2. Niccolò di Bernardo dei Machiavelli (1469–1527), in his treatise, *The Prince*, challenged the prevailing idea that the stability of a state depended on the God-given power of a just, honest and virtuous ruler. He asserted that the career of Cesare Borgia showed the opposite to be the case.
3. George Julian Harney

and making... 'thoroughly democratic speeches'". I hope the Proletarians of England will give these bourgeois profit-mongers and blood-suckers the reception they deserve.

Why, the conduct of these middle class humbugs at their trumpery conference, was—without the Charter League job—enough to open the eyes of any sane man as to their real character. The only one among the lot worth his salt, is Dawson of Birmingham[1]—who is no 'Brummagem ware', but good stuff, seeing that he spoke out like a man on the property dodge, and the position of the agricultural labourers. A very little more would make that man one of us; and I have hopes of him. As a Unitarian parson, Mr Dawson *ought* to know a little about Christianity, and what tenets really *were* taught by the Nazarean proletarian.

Of the conduct pursued by Mr O'Connor, in burking the two letters of Julian Harney's—given in the June number of this periodical—containing, as its readers are aware, a straightforward, energetic defence of the proletarian cause against the vile insinuations of Clark, and Co., and their 'honourable' parliamentary and financial employers, I shall not speak. That conduct has already been judged by the Chartist public.[2] I hope Mr O'Connor is not influenced by a hankering after the reputation of a 'respectable reformer'. Any such folly would fix him like a man attempting to sit between two stools—since to be the 'faithful and uncompromising advocate' of the proletarian cause, and a friend of the 'highly respectable influential gentlemen' composing the Executive Council of the National Parliamentary and Financial Reform Association, is an absolute impossibility. A proletarian leader, the friend of bourgeois profit-mongers! A people's champion, the friend of the most deadly and truculent among the people's foes! A hollow truce, but no sincere alliance, is all that can ever exist between a consistent proletarian champion and the leaders of that class which, more than all the other 'influential and respectable' classes of society put together, uses up the proletarian for its own purposes.

---

1. George Dawson (1821–1876) was a Birmingham preacher and social reformer who in 1845 abandoned a Baptist ministry for a new position at a Unitarian church.

2. 'Burking' is to suppress or dispatch without leaving marks of violence, following the example of William Burke, hanged in Edinburgh in 1829 for supplying bodies to anatomy schools in Edinburgh after having first smothered his victims.

A Bird's Eye View of the Glorious British Constitution

Democratic Review, September 1850

"Not to know", says Cicero, "what happened before we were born, is to remain always children; for, what were the life of man did he not combine present events with the recollection of past ages!"[1] In my opinion, one of the chief uses of History is, as an antidote to humbug. The study of history is a specific, or universal medicine, for all kinds of cant and twaddle about the wisdom of our ancestors, veneration of the Past with its admirable institutions, and the like; for the records of nations show that civilisation is by no means an invariable quantity. It is a fact which has incessantly changed its value and aspect with the lapse of time. The advocates of the past, therefore, might justly be required to point out the particular phasis of civilisation to which they refer, as the most excellent among its incessant fluctuations.[2] The *whole* past cannot be so admirable and vener-

---

1. Marcus Tullius Cicero (106–43 BCE) was a leading statesman during the decline and fall of the Roman Republic. Although he had very few original ideas, Cicero's style of artificial, convoluted oratory was emulated by the British ruling class, whose sons had it forced down their throats by despotic Latin schoolmasters. Following the assassination of Julius Caesar, which he approved of, Cicero was proscribed as an enemy of the state and murdered by supporters of Mark Anthony.
2. In this essay Macfarlane employs a Marxian critique of what was to become known as the 'Whig Theory of History'. Whig historians

able as they pretend, for the ages that have vanished contradict each other quite as much as the present contradicts them all. In what particular phasis of civilisation were the nature and destiny of man so explained and accomplished, that henceforth he has nothing to do but to fold his hands and remain, like the Indian Buddha, in a state of eternal repose? If this question cannot be answered with respect to Mankind, as little can it be answered with respect to any particular nation—for example, the British. Wisdom of our ancestors? No doubt they were wise in their day and generation, but *their* day was not *ours*. The wisdom of *which* set of ancestors? Of the Saxons? Then we shall make sad havoc in the wisdom of the Anglo-Normans, whose opinion on things in general were widely different again from those entertained by men under the Tudors. The wisdom of the Puritans? perhaps, all things considered, the most logical and least stupid of all our multifarious ancestors; yet I shudder to think what would then become of the *Stuarts* and their adherents: not to mention the *"worldly and profane"* wisdom of Dutch William, and the treacherous, mean, sneaking, rascally aristocrats who placed him on the throne.[1] The wisdom of George III and Lord North?[2] *Such* wisdom is questionable, seeing that the most memorable deed accomplished by *these* respected ancestors was the loss of the American colonies through an amount of obstinacy and stupidity unparalleled in the annals of the human race.

Amid this chaos of conflicting 'ancestor-wisdom', one is lost in admiration! Ought it not to be made law that every 'true-hearted Briton' should adopt the maxims of his respected ancestors by

---

such as Henry Hallam and Thomas Babington Macaulay argued that the seed of Liberty was planted with the Magna Carta in 1215; and then grew through the Reformation, and the Revolutions of the seventeenth-century, until finally flowering with the Parliamentary Reform Bill of 1832.

1. William of Orange (1650–1702) was Stadtholder of the United Provinces of the Netherlands from 1672. In 1688 leading English oligarchs, who were opposed to the Catholic absolutism of James II, invited William to invade England and overthrow James. William's 'Glorious Revolution' succeeded and he was crowned along with his wife Mary in 1689.

2. George III ruled until 1810, when his madness became permanent and his son—later George IV—took over as Prince Regent. Frederick, Lord North was Prime Minister 1770–1782.

turns, and give the wisdom of each epoch a fair trial? Seriously, my proletarian brothers, it would be extremely ludicrous to hear the upholders of established injustice talk of the *"glorious British constitution, admirable institutions, of our venerable forefathers"*, and the like, were it not that all this sickening twaddle is emitted with a purpose, namely, to deceive the people as to the real origin of the present state of things. It may suit the private purposes of the haughty descendants of Norman William and his horde of brigands—the purposes of those noble offshoots from royal harlots, whose fingers are in every man's pocket—the purposes of the coronetted Shylocks of the Stock Exchange—to promulgate endless absurdities on this subject; but the people would do well to think twice of the matter before believing whatever is told them by those whose interest it is to keep them ignorant of the truth.

When did this boasted constitution make its first appearance? Who were its originators? If the idea of a constitution be opposed to that of despotism, I presume it is so, because a constitution means a form of government which is based upon the *assent of the governed*, then history ought to present traces of this assent having been attained: in other words, *the whole community*, being now under the operation of this precious constitution, must in past ages have concurred in its fabrication. British history, however, on being interrogated, gives a very different account of the matter. The sacred and sacramental formula, which expresses the glorious British constitution, is 'King, Lords, and Commons'. Let us tear the veil from this aristocratic holy of holies, and look, with our profane and plebeian eyes, on what we find there. Let us analyse this mysterious formula, and ascertain what is the real meaning of it, if indeed it *has* any rational meaning. Our monarchy and aristocracy date from the year 1066. A hostile army then encamped on the soil of England; its chiefs obtained allotments of land proportionate to their rank and services (see Doomsday Book) on military tenures, which bound them together in one vast feudal system. In order to preserve amicable relations amongst these warrior-chiefs, they were often convoked by their general, whom they styled in their language *Roi*, to hold a consultation upon their affairs, which affairs were chiefly how to keep 'these base Saxon dogs' in proper subjection to their rulers and feudal superiors by divine right, and to wring from these slaves or *'subjecti'* the fruits of their labour. The lineal descendants of these mail-clad Norman barbarians are the hereditary legislators of England, and as they were originally the companions and equals of the General, they are now the peers of the king, and have privileges. The bulk of the nation, namely, the Saxons, were regarded after the conquest *'come gens taillable et corvéable à mercie'*—taxable, and forced to do taskwork, at the will of their masters. There is almost no mention of the vanquished for some time after the Conquest, except in Anglo-Norman characters as 'serfs, villains, colons', etc., who could acquire no property, and were sold along with houses, cattle, and farm implements, as belonging to the ground—*'vêtement de la terre'*.

In the year 1295, by the 23rd Act of Edward I, a certain number of burghs, arbitrarily selected as the most wealthy, were required to send deputies to the council of the King and his peers. That is the first appearance of the English *Tiers Etat*, or Third Estate, in the sacramental and sacred formula, 'King, Lords, and Commons', which so well expresses the spirit of our admirable and venerable institutions! And a very scurvy and scaly appearance it was too—one of the scurviest recorded in universal history; for these burgher deputies were summoned before the supreme court of aristocracy merely for the purpose of declaring how much the inhabitants of their respective townships could pay without being utterly ruined. From this it appears that the wisdom of the hereditary legislators in Anglo-Norman times, actually reached the sublime height of *not* killing the goose that laid the golden egg. If the landowners of these times would only take a lesson from this profound wisdom of their venerable forefathers, and refrain from *utterly* ruining the agricultural population! But it is perhaps too much to expect that men should be as wise, not to say *wiser*, than their respected ancestors; and the notion that the civilised world has gained anything from six hundred years of life and experience is quite fallacious, not to say atheistical, seditious, and illegal! After settling what their constituents were to pay, the deputies were dismissed, without being allowed to take part in the subsequent legislative measures of the Norman king and his peers, or equals. The expense attending these deputations was so onerous for the burghs selected as the victims of royal avarice, that, according to Hume, *"no intelligence could be more disagreeable to any borough than to find that they must elect, or to any individual than that he was elected"*.[1] Statutes were repeatedly enacted, especially by Richard II, to oblige boroughs to send deputies to parliament. After this first scurvy appearance of the Commons of England, in the sacred and inviolable formula descriptive of our glorious constitution, some two hundred years elapsed before they took courage to express an independent opinion, even on the money matters they were convoked to arrange. In 1509 the Commons first refused a subsidy by the mouth of Thomas Morus.[2]

Hitherto, I have looked in vain for the *"admirable balance of powers which forms so distinguishing a feature in our venerable constitution"*. In itself an absurdity, for a state of equilibrium or of rest, not of motion, is what results from the action of 'equally balanced powers', and at this rate the government of the county would stand still. Is this chimerical characteristic of our glorious constitution to be found later, for example in the 17th century, when the Commons cut off the king's head, and kicked the Lords to the devil? An odd balance of power, *that*!

In subsequent centuries, down to our own times, I can find no trace whatever of a *constitution*, though plenty of evidence exists as to the despotism exercised by one or two classes of society towards the mass of the nation. In a word, the 'glorious British constitution' is a chimera, a nonentity, existing only in the fond imaginations of those brainless gulls who take his Grace of Richmond[3] to be a new fifth evangelist, and whose wits (if ever they had any) have gone a wool gathering with Mr Ferrand and his wool league.[4]

The 'glorious British constitution' is the collective epithet for the present system of class legislation, and it simply means the glorious British Joint Stock Company for fleecing the starving producers of their last penny, that the dominant classes may exist in luxury and idleness. All the so-called 'reforms' have only

---

1. David Hume, *The History of England*, Vol. II, London: Christie and Son, 1819, p. 267.
2. Sir Thomas More (1478–1535), councillor to Henry VIII and Lord Chancellor from October 1529 to 16 May 1532.
3. General Charles Gordon Lennox, 5th Duke of Richmond (1791–1869), was an ultra-Tory and opponent of Catholic emancipation.
4. William Busfeild Ferrand (1809–89), MP for Knaresborough, was a member of Disraeli's 'Young England' Party, which espoused a paternalist 'Social Toryism'. In 1850 Ferrand launched a Farmers Wool League to boycott imported cotton.

been quarrels between the two ruling classes—between the 'landed and manufacturing interests'—as to who should have the greater share of the plunder. The Reform Bill and the League[1] were nothing else than battles fought by a set of hungry wolves and a set of hungry vultures over a carcase—the vultures, being the stronger of the two, prevailed. The question at issue was, which party should have the picking of it. The propriety of devouring the carcase at all? Such a question could evidently never occur to wolves or vultures.

From the earliest dawn of civilisation, from the first formation of society among the Caucasian races of man, we see nothing else going on than the struggles between classes or castes. In Hindostan and Egypt—the cradles of modern culture—we find class domination existing as a prominent, palpable, unmistakeable fact. It has continued to be an historical fact down to our own times, under the almost infinite variety, obtaining in the aspects and degrees of civilisation; and the battles of the social castes form the narrative of history. There is a difference between the Pariah of India, or the embalmer, swineherd, and other hereditary outcasts of Egypt; or the slave, whose testimony could legally be received by the polished Athenians only when extorted from him by the rack; or the slave who was thrown alive into fishponds to fatten carp for the supper of his Roman master; or the serf of the middle ages, who, like a dog, wore a collar round his neck with his master's name on it. There is a difference between these men and that of the modern proletarian in civilised, *Christian, enlightened* England. But the position of the wages slaves, even with the advantage of an invisible but glorious constitution, are, in reality, no better than that of any other kind of slaves who preceded them. For choice, *I* would prefer being thrown into a pond to feed carp, on the Roman plan, to being left to die by inches of starvation, in a filthy hole, unfit for a beast to live in—on the modern plan of "*free trade, supply and demand, unlimited competition, commercial crisis, slack time, reduction of wages*", and all the other cant of middle-class profitmongers and Malthusian economists of the Manchester school. That, however, is a matter of taste.

---

1. Anti-Corn Law League

Red Republican

June 1850 to November 1850

Chartism in 1850...

Red Republican, **22 June 1850**

... is a different thing from Chartism in 1840.[1] The leaders of the English Proletarians have proved that they are true Democrats, and no shams, by going ahead so rapidly within the last few years. They have progressed from the idea of a simple political *reform* to the idea of a *Social Revolution*. Returning lately to this country, after an absence of some years, I was agreeably surprised by this fact. *"What, old Mole! workest thou i' the earth so fast?"*[2] The spirit of

---

1. The Chartist movement was founded in 1838, when the six-point People's Charter was drawn up by the London Working Men's Association and the Birmingham Political Union. The six points were: A vote for every man over the age of 21; Secret ballot; No property qualification for members of Parliament; Payment for MPs; Constituencies of equal size; Annual elections for Parliament.
   By 1850 the Chartists had presented three petitions to Parliament (1839, 1842 and 1848). All of them were rejected in the House of Commons vote. The National Charter Association was founded in July 1840 in Manchester following the collapse of the Chartist National Convention and the defeat of the Newport Rising the previous year. Although it initially had hundreds of branches and ten of thousands of members, by 1850 national membership was down to hundreds.
2. The 'old mole' analogy is probably inspired by Hegel's use of it in his writings on the revolutions in thought: *"Spirit often seems to have forgotten and lost itself, but inwardly opposed to itself, it is inwardly working ever forward (as when Hamlet says of the ghost of his father, 'Well said, old mole! canst work i' the ground so fast?') until grown strong in itself it bursts*

the age is abroad here too, in practical anti-speculative England, and is teaching the masses more than is contained in the Thirty-nine Articles, and quite another confession of faith than that of Westminster.[1]

New views of man's nature, his duties, or rights—for the terms are synonymous, or nearly so, my duties being the rights of others, and *vice versa*—have been opened up to us of late. The Holy Spirit of truth, which the Nazarean promised to his followers, as a guide on their weary pilgrimage towards the promised land—towards a pure Democracy, where freedom and equality will be the acknowledged birth-right of *every* human being; the golden age, sung by the poets and prophets of all times and nations, from Hesiod and Isaiah, to Cervantes and Shelley; the *Paradise*, which was never lost, for it lives—not backwards, in the infancy and youth of humanity—but in the future, as the bright prize destined for the ripe manhood of the human race; this spirit, I say, has descended now upon the multitudes, and has consecrated them to the service of the new—and yet old—religion of Socialist Democracy. A social revolution? Truly, these words are the death-knell of the present state of society. If society it may be called, where every man's hand is armed against his brother's life by a murderous competitive system, and by po-

---

asunder the crust of earth which divided it from the sun, its Notion, so that the earth crumbles away. At such a time, when the encircling crust, like a soulless decaying tenement, crumbles away, and spirit displays itself arrayed in new youth, the seven league boots are at length adopted." (Hegel's Lectures on the History of Philosophy, Section Three: Recent German Philosophy, E. Final Result.) In 1852, Marx, in *Eighteenth Brumaire of Louis Bonaparte*, uses the Hegelian mole metaphor ironically in describing how Louis Bonaparte disguised his coup d'etat of 1852 as a revolution: "*But the revolution is thoroughgoing. It is still traveling through purgatory. It does its work methodically... And when it has accomplished this second half of its preliminary work, Europe will leap from its seat and exult: Well burrowed, old mole!*"

1. The Thirty-Nine Articles of 1563, staked out a 'middle-ground' for the Church of England between Catholicism and Protestantism. Macfarlane would have taken particular exception to Article XXXVIII, which attacks the communistic tendencies of Anabaptism: "*The Riches and Goods of Christians are not common, as touching the right, title, and possession of the same; as certain Anabaptists do falsely boast. Notwithstanding, every man ought, of such things as he possesseth, liberally to give alms to the poor, according to his ability.*"

A bill containing the six points is delivered to Lord John Russell, the Prime Minister. Punch, 1848.

litical institutions, which base the wealth and prosperity of one monopolist class of landlords and moneylords, upon the misery and degradation of the souls and bodies of the producing millions. What is the present position of the Chartist Party? We are agreed with the Red Republicans, or Socialist-democrats of other countries, as to the *end*. But what means are at our disposal for the accomplishment of this end? Who are our enemies, and how can we fight them to the best advantage? Our enemies—the enemies of the British Proletarians, whether of the manufacturing or agricultural districts—are all the other classes of society put together. Society, in the exercise of political rights and possessing a monopoly of social advantages—is defined by the gigantic fiction of a *"glorious British constitution"*, and time honoured humbug of our ancestors, to be *"Kings, Lords, and Commons"*. That is, a ministry and two Houses of Parliament. *"The sovereign of these realms"*, being notoriously a mere puppet in the hands of a profligate aristocratic clique; which, under the names of a Conservative or a Whig administration—thimbleriggs majorities in Parliament, and uses up the Proletarians for its own profit and that of the middle-classes, who support the system because they share the plunder. I say, *one* aristocratic clique, under various denominations, governs this country. With regards to the Proletarians, the policy of Whigs and Conservatives, has always been identical. If we are refused the franchise, and are made the Pariahs of the civilization we produce, the outcasts of the very society whose existence we render possible, the slaves of the classes we uphold in comfort and luxury in which we are forbidden to share; though, as *our* creation, we certainly have the best right to it—if we are to continue subject to the dominion of laws regarding *our* labour, food, education, and in fact, *our* whole existence—in the making of which we are allowed no voice—and for protest against which we are to be imprisoned, and outlawed, and sent like felons to penal colonies—then, I say, it is little matter whether the Government which acts towards the producers after this fashion, call itself Whig or Tory, or whether *"the red tape talking machine"* at the head thereof be called Russell or Wellington, Grey or Graham.[1] An hereditary aristocratic clique, sup-

---

1. Lord John Russell, Liberal Prime Minister; Duke of Wellington, commander-in-chief of the army; Sir George Grey, Liberal Home Secretary; and Sir James Graham, opposition Peelite Conservative.

ported by the financial aristocracy of the middle classes, and by the priests of a bloated and corrupt church, self-styled a Christian one; an hereditary House of Peers, with a Bench of Bishops, and a House of *Commons*—God save the mark! appointed by an electoral body of some eight hundred thousand, out of a population of some twenty-eight millions—such is the governing power of Great Britain—such is society, *within* the pale of the Constitution. And *without* the pale, stands the producing section of society, in an attitude very hostile to those of the other camp. We have outlived the two great Middle Class bubbles—the Reform Bill[1] and the League—and we see that there is no help to be expected from the Bourgeoisie. The *"Reformers"* who try to burk the Ten Hours' Bill;[2] who refuse to listen to any proposal for investigating the condition of the journeymen working 18 hours a day at unhealthy trades; who pay a Chartist renegade to stir up dissension in the Chartist camp, and traduce the motives of the most efficient among the Proletarian leaders, for the purpose of bringing them into discredit with the people; such Parliamentary and Financial Reformers can only be reckoned among the deadliest of the people's enemies. No thanks to these men and their base tools, that the admirable good sense, the instinctive rectitude, of the people, saved them from the snare; that those working men whom *"Sir Joshua Walmsley would not buy at any price"*, had discrimination enough to see through him and his hired apostate, by whose means he thought to hinder the reorganisation of Chartism, and to divide the Proletarians into contending sections, to be driven hither and thither like so many sheep, at the will and pleasure of Messrs. Cobden, Bright, and Co. For what do these men take us? For fools, I suppose, who are willing to thrust our

---

1. The Reform Act of 1832 granted seats in the House of Commons to the large cities that had sprung up during the Industrial Revolution, and abolished 'rotten boroughs' whose tiny electorates could be bought or intimidated. The Act increased the size of electorate from about 500,000 to 800,000—out of a British and Irish population of 25 million.

2. The Ten Hours Act of 1847 was passed to restrict the hours worked by women and children in factories. In February 1850, the Act was effectively repealed when a group of manufacturers accused of violating it were acquitted by the Court of Exchequer. A new Act was passed in August 1850, which fixed a 10½ hour working day for and children.

Robert Owen

Lord John Russell

hands a *third time* into the fire, having twice got nothing for our pains but burnt fingers. Had they the power this *Bright collection* of sleek financial hypocrites—they would treat us precisely as the middle-class order-mongers do our Proletarian brothers in France. What tub for the whale will these Free Trade and big loaf gentry throw out at the next commercial crisis? Without the support of the Proletarians, the Financial Reformers will find it impossible to carry any of their pet measures, or to satisfy their ancient grudge against the hereditary aristocracy; and the Proletarians will be mad indeed if they do not make the Six Points the condition of that support. Our reforming middle-class *friends*—wolves in sheep's clothing—would then be obliged to bolt *"the entire animal"*, and should they choke on the bristles, why—the Chartists would not die of grief for the sad event. But in order to be in a position to profit by coming events, it is necessary above all things to be unified. In my opinion, we English Proletarians never will do anything unless we apply the principle of *Centralization* to the management of our affairs. How comes it that our French brothers have done so much compared with us? *Because they are organized into one compact mass*, which, under the guidance of competent leaders, moves, like an army of well-disciplined soldiers, steadily onward to a given point. *That* is the reason of it. Frenchmen have the instinct of military discipline. We, on the other hand, carry the Saxon principle of the local management of affairs, and the infinitesimal division of interests, too far. Absolutely this will not do in fighting a battle. I should like to see London become for Britain what Paris is for France; viz: the centre of a Social Propaganda, the focus of Democratic agitation, the crater of the revolutionary volcano. But, at present, the Democratic interest in London is *split up into too many sections*.

We have the Executive Council of the National Charter Association, then the Society of Fraternal Democrats, the Social Reform League, the followers of Owen,[1] and perhaps half a dozen other sections or sectaries, differing upon minor points perhaps—but all agreeing as to the fundamental principles of Democracy and *the necessity which exists for a radical change in the condition of the people*. Now, why not coalesce? I should desire *above all things* to see the Fraternals, and also the Social Reformers, merged into the National Charter Association. For I am firmly

---

1. Robert Owen, socialist 'utopian' (1771–1858)

persuaded that this splitting up of the Democratic power into so many centres of action, is highly injurious to the Democratic interest. The working-men are at a loss to choose between so many Democratic Societies, and the activity of the Proletarian leaders is too severely taxed by having so great a multiplicity of details to attend to. In a word, *there is a waste of power.* A man, by concentrating his whole energy upon one thing at a time, will do a greater amount of work, and do it better—than he would by doing half a dozen different things at the same time. The Charter Association ought to be made the centre of the Democratic movement for two reasons. first, Chartism is already a familiar idea to the masses in this country, it has a firm hold upon their affections, and very justly so, for the Six Points are their Gospel of Freedom, to them the good tidings of great joy. Second, the enactment of the Charter—nay, of the one point, Universal Suffrage—would be the *political* emancipation of the producers; and I believe all sections of *real* Reformers are now agreed, that political reform must *precede* all attempts to improve the condition of the people, whether physically or intellectually. The *other classes* of society are not going to do anything to benefit the Proletarians. Are we to expect salvation at the hands of two such humbugs as my lords Ashley and Russell, with their hypocritical pretences about *"improving the condition of the poor?" "Do men gather grapes from thorns, or figs from thistles?"*[1] asked of old the Galilean carpenter; a man who could strike the nail on the head, better than most. I would especially, and most earnestly, intreat our friends, *the followers of Owen*—to consider this matter. Why is it, that with all their expenditure of time and money, they have never yet been able to put any of their Social Theories *into practice?* For the same reason that all the attempts of the Saint-Simonians in France, to improve the *social condition* of the people, failed most signally under the monarchy there.[2] The battle be-

---

1. Matthew 7:16: *"Ye shall know them by their fruits. Do men gather grapes of thorns, or figs of thistles?"*

2. Henri de Saint-Simon (1760–1825), saw the principal antagonism in modern society as between 'workers' and 'idlers'. Engels writes in *Socialism: Utopian and Scientific* (1880): *"... who was to lead and command? According to Saint-Simon, science and industry. But science, that was the scholars; and industry, was, in the first place, the working bourgeois, manufacturers, merchants, bankers... but they were still to hold, vis-à-vis of the workers, a commanding and economically privileged position. The bankers*

tween the classes composing society must be fought out first, before the Democratic and Social Republic can be organized. The first step to be taken for the benefit of a slave, is to set him free. Strike off his fetters, *then* you may feed him, clothe him, educate him, and otherwise *"improve his condition"*. *"Give me a fulcrum for my lever"*, said Archimedes, *"and I will move the world"*. A skilful engineer will fix upon *one* centre of motion, and from that single point, bring all his available power to bear upon the obstacle to be overcome. So, in my opinion, ought the English Democrats to do. The Social Reformers and the Fraternal Democrats cannot act until their hands be united; they can do nothing towards the *practical realization* of their social theories, until the Charter be Law. By uniting their funds with the Tract Fund of the Charter Association, they might have the advantage of the existing Chartist machinery of lecturers, places of meeting, etc., etc., for carrying on a Propaganda of Social ideas, much more extensive and efficient than they could do by their own unaided, isolated efforts. Such a Democratic Propaganda by means of lectures and the distribution of tracts, to be carried out on a large scale *by the united energy of the whole Democratic interest*, is highly necessary at present, especially in the *agricultural districts*. And thus, from one individual centre of Democratic action, a double movement might be carried on; viz: a crusade for the Charter as a merely political reform, and a veritable revolutionary and social Propaganda; and that too without distracting the attention of the people by the claims of so many Democratic Societies. I invite the attention of my Democratic brothers towards this subject.

---

especially were to be called upon to direct the whole of social production by the regulation of credit." Marshall Berman, in *All That is Solid Melts Into Air*, says that in Goethe's later writings his Faustian vision merges with Saint-Simonian socialism. Saint-Simonian scientists and engineers came up with various schemes for development on a vast, global scale. As Macfarlane points out, the schemes made little progress under Louis Phillipe. But, Louis Bonaparte, who was about to seize power in France, subsequently utilized the 'practical schemes' of the Saint-Simonians. *"They organized the French railway system; established the Credit Mobilier, an international investment bank to finance the merging world energy industry, and realized on of Goethe's fondest dreams, the Suez Canal."* Marshall Berman, *All That is Solid Melts into Air*, pp. 72-74.

The Red Flag in 1850

Red Republican, 13 July 1850

"*The red flag is the banner of the future*". A truth this, which all our sham reforming friends would do well to consider. In the category of sham reformers I include all the advocates of merely surface changes; of alterations in the form of government; of that shifting of power from the hands of one class into those of another, which yet leaves the old principle of class legislation as the basis of the social system. Whether such reformers be the bold 'Parliamentary and Financial' supporters of the bourgeois supremacy, or persons who pretend to be the friends of the Proletarians whose very lifeblood they suck—or who have sat still, as it were, on the rock of Chartist tradition, (like so many Chartist Robinson Crusoes) while the 'still vexed Bermoothes' of Democracy has kept surging past them, bearing men, facts, ideas, onwards to the future—matters not.[1] Consciously or unconsciously, all merely political reformers are Shams—Quacks, who attempt to cure a cancer which is eating away the very vitals of the patient, by exhibiting the remedies appropriate to a skin disease. If the principle according

---

1. The Bermoothes are the Bermuda Islands. In Shakespeare's *The Tempest*, Act I, Scene 2, Ariel says:

   Safely in harbour is the king's ship;
   in the deep nook, where once
   Thou call'dst me up at midnight to fetch dew
   From the still-vex'd Bermoothes, there she's hid

to which society is constituted be left untouched, the outward form of government is of small consequence. Wherever 'Society' means nothing else than a joint stock company for the using up of man by man, the enslaving of one class for the benefit of the others—such an arrangement of things cannot be affected by merely political reforms. This will be made evident by a glance at the three countries, Russia, England, and the United States. In Russia and other Slavonic countries, the agricultural population—the peasants—are the serfs, the beasts of burden. In England, the producers generally are the class used up by the hereditary and financial Aristocracy, the landlords and moneylords. And these White Slaves of England are worse off than their Slavonic brethren, or their ancestors, the serfs of the middle ages, in one respect—namely, the yoke which galls them is impalpable, so to speak, it is *"the force of circumstances"*. Wages are low, the burden of indirect taxation is heavy, the necessaries of life are proportionably dear—but these things cannot be helped. *"We are starving, give us food for a fair day's work". "Impossible, my dear fellows! There is a glut in the market from over speculation; how can we give you wages, when we have no outlet for our goods? We can't sell, and you must be content to starve; unless charitable people keep you alive by means of soup kitchens, etc., till trade gets better, and we want you again in our mills. But don't look sulky; there are prisons enough for starving vagabonds who so much as hint at changing the existing order of things".*

In America, women generally and coloured people are enslaved and used up by the free and enlightened citizens of that sham Republic.[1] And if the results of class legislation be not so visible there, in the shape of misery and crime, as they are in Europe, it is because the Yankees have an immense extent of fertile country with a sparse population. But the same causes must ultimately produce the same effects, and it is a question of time merely for Yankeedom. That El Dorado of the middle-class leaders, the be-praised of sleek Mr Bright, and the *beau ideal* of practical Mr Cobden, is in a fair way of becoming another England,

---

1. The feminist movement in America came in existence when white women campaigning against slavery decided to fight for their own freedom as well. The most revolutionary event of 1848 in America had been the Women's Rights Convention at Seneca Falls, New York. At the time Macfarlane was writing this movement was organizing for the first National Woman's Rights Convention, which met at Worcester, Massachusetts, October 23–24, 1850, with 900 delegates.

presenting the same hideous contrasts of Luxury and Starvation, of Rich and Poor. The absolute despotism which obtains in Russia now, as it did in Europe during the middle ages, obtains in England and America also, in spite of all *political* Reforms. Class domination has been filtered through Constitutional Media, getting less repulsive, perhaps, with each filtration to the superficial observer—"*small by degrees and beautifully less*"[1]—irresponsible power has been shifted from one class to another; in one country its possession depends on the accidents of birth and wealth; in another, on those of colour and sex; but in every country the odious fact remains, that some class of society treat the rest as Pariahs, putting them without the pale of civilization and its advantages. We want no merely political Reforms. Let us have done with Shams. We are sick of them. Did the Reform Bill and the League give us abundant food, and airy gardens, and clean well ordered houses, instead of starvation in filthy cellars? Did these middle-class bubbles give us education and the *leisure to profit by it*, instead of hopeless, debasing ignorance and ceaseless toil? We want no *third* Sham. We want a *Social Revolution*, that we may live like men and not like beasts; that our wives and children may not die of hunger by inches before our eyes; that our sons may not grow up stunted and deformed by premature and excessive labour; that our daughters may not become prostitutes at twelve and thirteen years of age, in order to eke out their scanty means of subsistence by the wages of abominable vice. We, the veritable people, the Proletarians, desire a Social Revolution; that is, a *radical change in our social condition*, because *we* produce the boasted fabric of English greatness and English civilization. Have *we*, then, not a right to share in the blessings of that civilization? Are the bees of England to work incessantly, producing honey for a set of lazy drones? No, my Proletarian brothers, this iniquitous system must be abolished. Who is to do it? The Red Republicans, if you except their guidance. Willingly, indeed, or unwillingly, you must follow in their wake; for the Genius of Universal History has at length resolved, that the Gospel of Equality and

---

1. From the poem, 'Henry and Emma', by Matthew Prior (1664–1721)

    No longer shall the body aptly laced,
    From thy full bosom to thy slender waist,
    That air and harmony of shape express,
    Fine by degrees, and beautifully less'.

Fraternity, hid under the ruins of eighteen centuries, shall be brought to light in the nineteenth; and *"The RED flag is the banner of the Future"*. *"Bread and work, the Organisation of Labour"*, these words contain the law of the new Epoch, they are the handwriting on the wall, which startles kings and base priests of an idolatrous mammon-worship, from their luxurious feasts and fancied securities. We, English Red Republicans, may do much to hasten the advent of this epoch; but it will only be by enlightening the masses as to their actual position and their social rights, for their ignorance on these points is indeed lamentable. Only the other day I saw in the Manchester newspapers, that a set of working men at Bradford had collected £60, in pence, towards the Industrial Exhibition of 1851—£60, in hard-earned pence, to make the condition of the producers still worse than it is already.[1] £60, to help to bring an immense quantity of foreign manufactures into the home market, to compete with British goods, produced under a high pressure system of taxation. £60, as a subscription from a set a working men, towards a reduction of prices, and consequently of wages too! £60, in a word, to increase and develop that ruinous competitive system, which enables the capitalist to prey upon the producer and use him up, body and soul! Heavens and Earth! one is struck dumb before folly like this. Universal Suffrage? The Six Points? *Instruments* merely, valuable or worthless, according to the use made of them. What would be the use of giving Universal Suffrage to a set of donkeys like those wise men of Gotham, I mean of Bradford, who walk deliberately into every middle-class dodge, and subscribe their pence at the beck of Messrs. Cobden, Bright, Walmsley, and Co.?

Yet, in spite of the ignorance and folly of those who *ought* to give us hearty support, since we are fighting *their* battle; in spite of the open hostility of all *"respectable people"*, of all the adherents of the established order of things—from the Austro-Russian Aristocrats and their *"highly influential"* stamped organs, down to the Little Charter Professors of Parliamentary and Financial humbug—in spite of all this, our position in 1850 is by no means a discouraging one. We, English Socialist-democrats, may be the *"ragged fringe upon the Red Republican cap, the bastard of the Mountain"*, as the sapient *Mr Boz* has been pleased to denominate us,

---

1. 'The Great Exhibition of the Works of Industry of all Nations', was held in Hyde Park, London, May to October 1851

but we are also somewhat more than this.[1] We are *"Chartists and something more"* even than *that*. Chartism and Red Republicanism must henceforward be considered as synonymous terms; to judge from the Executive Council lately chosen by the Chartist party. And what is Chartism? Why, I think if the stones of Kersal Moor, and Peep Green, and Kennington Common, could find a voice, it would appear that Chartism is something very much resembling the hope and aspiration of a majority of the working men of England.[2] *Chartism under the red flag,* is a vindication of the Claims of Labour; it is the enunciation of the *"Gospel of Work"*; the assertion, that the fustian jacket and the paper caps are infinitely more honourable emblems than the ermine robe and the coronet. The symbols of the active brain and the cunning hand, of Man's mastery over inanimate Nature, that of Knowledge and Power, set forth in the old Oriental myths as being a link in the chain which connects Humanity with Deity—*"and Elohim said 'Lo! Adam has become like one of us'"*[3]—the symbols of Labour, I say, are incomparably more honourable than the symbols of the force and fraud, which, during the dark ages laid the foundation of the present power and wealth of aristocrats and hereditary legislators. Yes, our cause, 'Chartism in 1850'—is the cause of the veritable People of England; it is the cause of the producers, and the battle of this one enslaved class is the battle we fight, but it must be fought under the *Red* flag, for that is the symbol of the new Epoch, *"the banner of the Future"*.

The task given us at present, is to rally our brother Proletarians *en masse* round this flag, by means of a Democratic and So-

---

1. 'Mr Boz' is Charles Dickens. In his 'Preliminary Word' to *Household Words*—a *Weekly Journal*, launched March 1850, Dickens promises his readers that: *"No mere utilitarian spirit, no iron binding of the mind to grim realities, will give a harsh tone to our Household Words"*; and says of radical competitors, such as the *Red Republican*: *"Some tillers of the field into which we now come, have been before us, and some are here whose high usefulness we readily acknowledge, and whose company it is an honour to join. But, there are others here—Bastards of the Mountain, draggled fringe on the Red Cap, Panders to the basest passions of the lowest natures—whose existence is a national reproach. And these, we should consider it our highest service to displace."* Household Words, Vol 1 No 1, London, 1850.
2. Kennington Common (London), Kersal Moor (Manchester) and Peep Green (Hartshead Moor) were sites of major Chartist mobilisations.
3. Genesis 3:22

cial Propaganda; an agitation for the *"Charter and something more"*. the present position of our affairs favours this line of action. We are getting re-organized, slowly but surely, and we are all the better for the Charter League dodge. It has taught us to distinguish false friends from real ones, apostates and traitors from honest men; and has put us on our guard against the villainous intrigues of the Middle-class leaders. Events too are looming on the political horizon, which will lead to results favourable to us, led as we are *now* by honest and intelligent men, who are both able and willing to take advantage of circumstances as they arise. In spite of the late ministerial majority of 46, it is pretty generally allowed that the present set of State Quacks will not be able to keep their ground much longer. Who is to succeed them? An Austro-Russian Protectionist Cabinet? I, for one, hope so. I am no friend of *moderates*, of *constitutionalism*, of half measures.

Neck or nothing, is my maxim. Do you fear the effect of such a change from rose-water, soft sawdering Whigs, to Tory knights of our foreign Brothers? It would have the highly beneficial effect of abridging their term of probation, by hastening the next revolutionary outbreak in Continental Europe. The Despots abroad, encouraged by their friends in England, would proceed to still greater extremities of tyranny than ever; and you know that if pressure be applied beyond a certain point, say on the safety valve of a boiler, that what the newspapers call *"a terrific explosion, accompanied by loss of life"*, inevitably ensues. Remember, that the triumph of the good cause in Italy was indefinitely postponed, not by the armies of physical force Despots, like those of Austria or Naples, but by the diplomatic cunning and smooth official trickery of Lord Palmerston's *constitutional* friend, the rascally King of Sardinia. In this country, the advent of the *"Cossacks"* to power, would afford Messrs. Cobden and Co. an opportunity of doing a little opposition business.

Between Free Traders and Protectionists, it would then be *"pull baker, pull devil!"*—and no mistake. And the result for us? Unquestionably good. For, *"when rogues fall out, honest men get their own"*—and if the Parliamentary and Financial Reform clique wish the support of the Producers, the price of the working men of England in the market of 1850, is *Universal Suffrage*, whether Sir Joshua Walmsley be willing to pay it or not. Hurrah, then for *"the Charter and something more!"* Hurrah for *"the Red Flag—the banner of the Future!"*

Fine Words (Household or Otherwise) Butter No Parsnips

Red Republican, 20 July 1850

The above moral reflection occurred to me on reading an article in the last monthly edition of *Dickens' Household Words*, wherein two poor little starving children, who stole a loaf of bread, and were sentenced by a Bow-street magistrate ("*a Daniel come to judgment*"[1]) to be whipped for this "*awful crime against society, property, and order*". Further, the writer relates divers particulars concerning the ragged schools in Westminster, tending to show that persons belonging to the offscourings of society—persons who, from their infancy, had been brought up in every kind of vice, are reclaimable with a little trouble, but that the *first condition* of that reformation is to give them the means of earning their living in an honest way. In the cases mentioned by this writer, this was done by sending the subjects of the experiment to Australia, where, by last accounts, they "*were doing well*". I daresay they "*were doing well*", in a country where the poor are not *altogether* thrust from the banquet of life by the rich; where the land, the common gift of God to all mankind, is not *altogether* monopolized by one land-owning class; where the honest man who only has his strength and skill to aid him in the struggle for existence, does not *altogether* become the prey of bourgeois profit-mongers, whose grand problem is—to get a maximum of

---

1. Shakespeare, The Merchant of Venice: Act 4, Scene 1:
    Shylock: *A Daniel come to judgment! yea, a Daniel!*
    O wise young judge, how I do honor thee!

work done for a minimum of wages. No doubt, any one, willing to work, would *"do well"* in a place like this. The remedy proposed by the above writer for the state of things he describes is—*National Education!* *"If a son asks bread from any of you that is a father, will he give him a stone?"*[1]

A *spelling-book* as a cure for hunger, was an amount of human absurdity, which evidently had not crossed the imagination of the Nazarean Teacher. *Words* are the panacea of the Whig Quacks and rosewater political sentimentalists of the Boz school. Education will do much, and a fit subject for its beneficent influences would have been the brutal, well-fed Dogberry who sentenced these starving children to be whipped; but Education will not satisfy the *animal* wants of man; the rule of three will not feed the hungry, or the *Penny Magazine* clothe the naked. How are the people of this country to be *fed?* That is the question. Not, how are the starving, homeless, hopeless wretches, dying by inches of cold and hunger, to be taught *"reading, writing and arithmetic"*.

Your lessons in morality will do much for men who must either starve or steal, for women who must go on the streets and drive a hideous traffic in their own bodies, to get a meal for their starving children! Rose-coloured political sentimentalists! All this is atrocious, inhuman humbug—and you know it. You boast much of the *"Charitable Institutions of England"*—I tell you the word charity is an insult, and your vaunted institutions are a mockery. Supposing you had the right—which you have *not*—of monopolizing the land, enslaving the producers, then giving them the bread which is their birthright as human beings, as a charity—God save the mark!—supposing you had the right of doing all this, I say, yet your *"Institutions"* are quite inadequate to relieve the tenth part of the hideous misery created and fostered by your vicious system of society. For a proof of this assertion, I need only point to Ireland—I need only turn to the columns of the *Morning Chronicle*—I need only refer to the accounts of inquests given by the Manchester newspapers, where I see every now and then such verdicts as—*"died of destitution"*; and while these facts exist, it is vain to talk of *"Charitable Institutions"*, and Sidney Herbert[2] schemes for transporting *"the distressed needle-*

---

1. Luke 11:11
2. Sidney Herbert (1810–1861), Peelite Conservative MP.

women of the metropolis" to other countries, in search of adequately paid employment they *ought* to have found at home.

Transport the lazy drones who eat up the honey; transport the landowners and the thimble-riggers of the Stock Exchange, and there would be bread enough and room enough *then*, for all *"our surplus population"*. How are the people of this country to be *fed*? That is the problem for solution. The Protectionists did not solve it. The Free-traders are not solving it. Rosewater, self-sawdering, sentimental Whigs talk of National Education. Meanwhile, the producers die of inches of hunger—pauperism, and its attendant—crime—are on the increase. The condition of *"moral England, the envy of surrounding nations"*, is in a fair way of becoming very unenviable under the Upas-tree of a *"glorious British Constitution and time-honoured Institutions of our ancestors"*. It is well *Time* honours them, for I think nobody else does, and time must be in his dotage if he does anything of the kind.

It has lately been said by the *Leader* that the writers in the *Red Republican* are *"violent, audacious and wrathfully earnest"*.[1] Ah my dear *Leader*, do you perceive that it is quite impossible for a *Red Republican*—that is a *sworn foe of existing social arrangements*—to be anything else than *"violent and audacious"*? Though he were to *"roar as gently as any sucking dove"*,[2] he would still be found *"violent"* by those who uphold the existing social system. For my part I

---

1. Thornton Leigh Hunt and George Henry Lewes, founders, in 1850, of *The Leader*, were associated with the Christian Socialist movement, along with Charles Kingsley (author of *The Water Babies*) and E. Vansittart Neale, a founder of the Working Men's College in London. At the time Macfarlane was writing for the Red Republican, Lewes's lover, George Eliot (Marian Evans) was working with him at the *Westminster Review* and contributing to the Leader under a pseudonym. Whilst there is no evidence that Macfarlane and Evans ever met, they had in common a deep interest in radical German philosophy: Evans had translated of *The Life of Jesus*, by David Strauss (and would later translate Lugwig Feuerbach's *Essence of Christianity*); Macfarlane translated Marx and a little bit of Hegel. Eliot's recent biographer, Karl Frederick, suggests it is possible that she met Marx in 1850, because Marx is known to have visited the offices of the *Westminster Review*, offering some translations of poetry by Ferdinand Freiligrath— which were rejected as too 'extreme'.

2. Shakespeare, *A Midsummer Night's Dream*: Act 1, Scene 2.

Bottom: ... *but I will aggravate my voice so that I will roar you as gently*

am proud of the epiphet—violent, and wrap myself in audacity, as in a mantle. Wrathfully earnest! I should think we are. Just about as much in earnest as our precursor, *"the Sansculotte Jesus"* was when He scourged the usurers and money-lenders, and *thimble-rigging stockbrokers* of Jerusalem out of that temple they *"had made a den of THIEVES"*. About as earnest as our Nazarean brother was, when—denouncing those who laid heavy burdens of the poor, whom they used up for their own profit, refusing to touch these burdens of their fainting oppressed brethren, with *"one of their little fingers"*, he exclaimed, *"Ye serpents! ye generation of vipers! how shall ye escape the damnation of Hell?"*[1] Yes, we are tolerably in earnest, in demanding that the Gospel of Christ shall no longer remain a dead letter; that the noble idea of Fraternity and Equality, first promulgated by the Galilean carpenter, shall at length be realized; that *"the ideal of justice and love, which we have long seen glittering above us should descend"* into the furrows where the toiling peasant stoops—into the workshops and mills where the pale artisan drags out the twelve and fourteen hours a day, that have made him so stunted, so deformed, and sickly a sample of humanity. We are certainly in earnest, inspired by the same spirit as Paul, who said, *"If any man be not willing to work, neither let him eat"*.[2] The present *"visible Church of Christ"* read this text corrected thus—*"If any man, kings, princes, state priests, and aristocrats—whether landed or financial—excepted, be not willing to work, neither let him eat; and those who are the hardest worked shall receive the smallest amount of food"*. *"For eighteen centuries"*, says an eloquent French professor, *"man has been satisfied with reading the Gospel; this is not enough; it is henceforth necessary that he should write it himself upon the surface of the earth, upon the brow of nations, upon sand, upon brass, in laws, institutions, and new charters. Every Christian nation ought to be an immortal evangelist"*.[3]

The idea of perfect Liberty, of Equality and Fraternity—the divine idea of love, incarnate in the gentle Nazarean, is the idea we earnestly worship. It freed itself from the dead weight of a lifeless Past in the days of Luther, bursting forth from under the

---

as any sucking dove;
I will roar you an 'twere any nightingale.

1. Matthew 23:33
2. Thessalonians 3:10
3. Source unkown.

accumulated rubbish of ages, like waters of life—like a fountain to refresh the wanderer fainting in desert places: it found an expression free from all symbols, sagas, and historical forms, in the *Declaration of the Rights of Man*, by Maximilian Robespierre, and in the immortal pages of [Rousseau's] *Contrat Social* and *Emile*.[1]

The next step in the development of this divine idea will be its practical realization: the Ethico-political regeneration of society, which our early oriental brothers, the proletarian suffers under the *Roman* despots, pictured as the second coming of that thorn-crowned Martyr, on Calvary; the reign of God's saints on earth. Sedition! Imprisonment! Transportation to penal settlements! Suppression of the *Red Republican*! Let them suppress it if they dare.[2]

We, the writers therein, will find other and quite as effectual modes of expressing our thought. We will go forth on the highways and byeways—by the roadside—in every mill and workshop we will preach the Rights and Wrongs of labour, from that text of Paul's—*"If any man be not willing to work, neither shall he eat"*. And should we be imprisoned or sent beyond seas, we will console ourselves by the reflection that the spirit of the age has no lack of fit organs to express its thought—that the work will not stand still, because a few workmen have been removed; we will rejoice that we have been found *worthy to suffer* for this divinest idea of Liberty, Equality, Fraternity—to be joined to its Martyrs and Apostles, that glorious band, gathered from all ages

---

1. The phrase *"accumulated rubbish of ages"* echoes Marx's words in the *German Ideology*, p. 95: "*this revolution is necessary, therefore, not only because the ruling class cannot be overthrown in any other way, but also because the class overthrowing it can only in a revolution succeed in ridding itself of all the muck of ages and become fitted to found society anew.*"

2. In November 1850, Marx learned from Chartist leader, Ernst Jones, that the *Red Republican* was being threatened with prosecution for not paying Stamp Duty. Marx wrote to Engels: "*The entire contents of [Harney's] paper are such as to make it liable to stamp duty. The government is merely waiting for its circulation to increase in order to nab him.*" Charles Dickens had been having similar trouble and proceedings against Dickens had been "*instituted solely as a precedent in respect of Harney. If he is arrested he may, besides the actual sentence, have to serve 20 years through being unable to produce securities.*" MECW Vol 38, p. 242.

The prosecution, however, did not materialise.

and nations—"*a peculiar people, a sacred priesthood*",[1]—the best and noblest of the human race.

---

1. Peter 2:9

Middle-class Dodges and Proletarian Gullibility in 1850
'A Penny Monument to Sir Robert Peel!'

Red Republican, 17 August 1850

Meetings of working men in Mechanics' Institution, presided over by civic dignitaries, to invite the co-operation of the proletarians in *"doing honour to the memory of an illustrious statesman"*. A working man's committee to receive proletarian subscriptions towards this *"laudable object!"* A letter from Mr Cobden, encouraging the producers to show *"their gratitude to the great man who had done so much good for them"*. *"Upwards of £21 subscribed by the operatives in the employment of Messrs. Salis, Schwebe, and Co. of Manchester, towards the Peel Monument"*. A nice collection of texts that—is it not?—from which to preach a Chartist sermon on middle-class dodges and proletarian gullibility! I am free to confess, that, however great may be the talent for sleight-of-hand tricks, however monstrous the humbug and hypocrisy of the bourgeois leaders, as displayed in their recent dealings with the Proletarians, yet the latter possess a proportionably great capacity for being deceived by these tricks—for swallowing that humbug. An immense fund of proletarian simplicity and credulity exists, as so much raw material, to be worked up for the private purposes of Messrs. Walmsley, Cobden, Bright and Co.; and to do these gentlemen justice, their assiduity is remarkable: there is no slack time with them. Dodge follows dodge—like Banquo's kings—in, apparently, interminable succession: whilst gaping crowds of *starving disenfranchised slaves* surround the stage, where these political charlatans and thimble-riggers play their tricks, and sell their nostrums to the fools who take the selfish dogmas of the Manchester school to be the Word of Life, and the Committee of the Parliamentary and Financial Reformers to be so many new Evangelists who preach salvation to the people. A spectacle, this, for gods and men—pity one could not follow Byron's pithy advice—

You've freed the Blacks
Now pray shut up the Whites![1]

For, save in Bedlam, I think a similar amount of folly and delusion is nowhere to be found. Ah! My good, easy, simply credulous, gullible, humbugged Proletarian brothers!—known to an admiring world as *"Conservative Operatives"*, subscribers to the Industrial Exhibition of 1851, to the Peel Monument, and generally, as the victims of bourgeois dodges—you certainly understand the *letter*, if not the *spirit*, of one text in the Christian gospel, *"To him that smiteth thee on the one cheek, turn the other one also; and from him that taketh away your mantle, withold not your vest also"*. Have you then not one spark of sense or of manliness in your composition? Did Nature, when she gave you *heads*, forget to put *brains* into them?

It would appear so. Did it never occur to you to ask the *meaning* of the term—*"Conservative Operative"*? The answer is obvious enough—a *"Conservative Operative"*, is a slave who hugs his chains out of stupidity or cowardice, no matter which. Every Proletarian who does not see and feel that he belongs to an enslaved and degraded class, is a fool; if he see, but dare not resent, his wrongs, he is a *contemptible coward*. Did you never think of asking your middle-class *friends*, why *you* should subscribe to the Industrial Exhibition of 1851? What benefits are the *producers* to obtain by so doing? I protest, I am open to conviction, if any one will show me the benefits that will arise to the *Proletarian* class, from this

---

1. Byron, *Don Juan*, LXXXII

   O Wilberforce! thou man of black renown,
   Whose merit none enough can sing or say,
   Thou hast struck one immense Colossus down,
   Thou moral Washington of Africa!
   But there's another little thing, I own,
   Which you should perpetrate some summer's day,
   And set the other half of earth to rights;
   You have freed the blacks—now pray shut up the whites.

Middle-class Dodges and Proletarian Gullibility 61

precious exhibition. You take these imaginary benefits, these advantages *in posse*, on the word of the middle-class leaders; because you believe—like the poor deluded simpletons you are—in the lip-sympathy, the empty professions of friendship made to you by these sleek bourgeois humbugs and profit mongers. They have certainly given you very convincing proofs of their *friendship*!

A man who refuses to let me share in the advantages he himself enjoys to satiety, and to give me back those of which he has unjustly deprived me, is my *friend*, is he? If he really be my friend, *let him show it in his actions*; or else be silent, and refrain from adding the guilt of hypocrisy and the meanness of telling lies, to the crimes of selfishness of injustice, and of spoliation. Your bourgeois *friends* refuse to give you Universal Suffrage, and the political economists of the Manchester school sneer contemptuously at the phrase *"Organization of Labour!"* that is, they refuse you a share in the political and social advantages they themselves enjoy. They refuse you the franchise, in order that you, the *tax-producers*, may have no control over the moneylords and landlords, who are the *tax-eaters*. I think it was Cobbett who said—if a man be too ignorant to have a vote, he ought to be considered too ignorant to pay taxes.[1] They refuse you a share of the products of *your own labour*, in order to monopolize the whole, and build up colossal fortunes upon the foundation of your sufferings and misery. What aspect, regarding labour, does the prevailing system of social arrangements present? Broadcloth and silk are woven by the pale, half-naked, squalid artisan, crouching fourteen and sixteen hours a day over his loom for a pittance barely sufficient to keep him from actual starvation. Houses like palaces, are built by the denizens of damp, filthy cellars unfit for human habitation. Rich fields of golden grain are sown and reaped by the labourer who gets scarcely enough of the coarsest food to satisfy his hunger, who lives in a hovel like a pigstye, and whose only resource is the workhouse when crippled by old age, or by the fever and rheumatism brought on by the privations and hardships to which he is incessantly exposed. Yet the men who refuse to take one step towards the abolition of this shameful, this disgustingly impudent, system of open spoliation, are your *friends*, are they? The men

---

1. William Cobbett (1763–1835) was Radical MP for Oldham 1832–35. His essays in the *Political Register* and *Rural Rides* were immensely popular.

who are incessantly occupied with schemes for the aggrandizement of their own particular caste, which they have the effrontery to call "*legislating for the benefit of the community*", are sincere in their professions of friendship for the Proletarians! You must be mad indeed, if you can, for a moment, believe such palpable absurdity as *that*. I tell you, these men are your deadliest enemies. I tell you that experience shows two things, which, unless you wilfully shut your eyes, you cannot avoid seeing: namely, that the organisation of labour is the only remedy for the sufferings of the producers; and that the *first step* towards the accomplishment of this end, is the enactment of the Charter. *Universal Suffrage* would place the power of making laws where it *ought* to be, viz., in the hands of the *producing* classes of society. We, who render the very existence of the nation possible, have certainly the best right to dispose of the products of our own toil, the work of our own hands; and a right to secure the *means of existence for ourselves*. You, my humbugged proletarian brothers, are a set of egregious and hopeless fools, if you expect help in this matter from your *friends* belonging to the "*middle and higher*" classes of society—help from any one *save yourselves*. Yes when the wolf lies down with the lamb, and beasts of prey change their nature, *then* perhaps will the antagonistic classes of society cease to prey on each other; the tax-consumers will cease using up the tax-producers; the landlords and moneylords will cease using up the Proletarians. The Organization of Labour, includes—amongst other things—the *abolition* of antagonistic castes or classes, by means of the total annihilation of the "*landed and manufacturing interests*", those two great joint-stock companies for robbing the producers of the just reward for their toil. This annihilation will be effected by declaring the land to be *national* property, and that rent is payable only to the state, by declaring *private* property in banks, railways, etc., to be at an end, and by everywhere substituting the principle of association and the just division of the products of labour, for the present system of unlimited competition and monopoly. Under the law of *direct and Universal Suffrage*, this interference of the State, for the purpose of securing the physical and moral well-being of all, through the operation of just and wise laws, *would be the people looking after their own affairs*. Which they certainly have the right of doing; I assert, in spite of all the cant about "*centralization*" and "*interference with the rights of property*"—just as much as each individual has the right of regulating the interior affairs of his own household, in order to provide for the wants of *all* the members of his family. Your *"free-trading big loaf" friends*, whether Manchester millowners, Liverpool shippers, or London stockbrokers and railway stags, understand all this extremely well. The moneylords and landlords may quarrel, like a horde of brigands, about the divison of the spoil, as they did at the time of the [1832] Reform Bill and the [Anti-Corn Law] League; but as to the question of *pillaging the producers*, they are wonderfully unanimous; and the gentlemen of the Parliamentary and Reform Association, resist Universal Suffrage as stoutly as my Lord John Russell himself. I have read the newspapers; and with these things before your very eyes, how comes it that you do not see the barefaced impudence of those aristocrats whether of the monied or landed faction, who ask you to disburse your hard-earned pence to Sir Robert Peel? *What*, I ask in God's name, did Sir Robert Peel ever do for the *Proletarians* of England, that they should honour his memory? Is it on account of the Currency Bill of 1819? By which he feathered his own nest pretty well, *at the expense of the taxpayers*. If, on *this* account, a Proletarian Monument to Peel, why not a Proletarian Temple to Hudson?[1] Why not a general Apotheosis and a new Proletarian Calender of all the Saints of Mammon-worship? I challenge any one to point to a single measure of Sir Robert Peel's that has really made the condition of the Proletarians better than it was before that measure became law. I would gladly acknowledge his claims on the gratitude of his suffering countrymen, but no such claims exist. His political career may be summed up in a single sentence: *he first patronized the landlords, then the moneylords, and left the Proletarians to shift for themselves.* You, Proletarian fools, who spent, or are going to spend, your hard-earned money on a monument in honour of a man whose whole life was devoted to the cause of your deadly enemies, be *consistent*! Bow down before the golden calf whatever shape it may assume! Kiss the feet of the tithe-gathering, mitred priests, who pretend to be the followers of the meek and lowly Jesus! Do homage to the whole host of Protectionist landowners, free-trading bourgeois profitmongers, Jewish money lenders,

---

1. George Hudson (1800–1871), MP for Sunderland 1845–59, and known as 'The Railway King', had control of over a thousand miles of railway by 1844. He was subsequently ruined by the disclosures of fraud and bribery of MPs.

thimblerigging fundholders, stockbrokers, and speculators, who are draining your very life-blood!

If you accept the present system of society without protest, and raise monuments to the man who did all in his power to uphold it—then you must go a step further, you must accept all the results of that system of social arrangements, all the consequences which logically follow from the principles of selfishness and class-legislation at the bottom of that system. Beside the Peel Monument and the Hudson Temple, you must raise altars to famine and pestilence, to physical suffering and moral degradation. You must worship the genius of misery and crime. You must rejoice at the approach of the typhus fever which rages in the unwholesome dwellings of the poor, and exult in the prostitution of your wives and daughters for a morsel of bread.

Democratic Organization

Red Republican, 17 August 1850:

In my article entitled 'Chartism in 1850', published in the first No. of this paper, I expressed the opinion that all the different sections of Social Reformers should coalesce and form but one body, for the twofold purpose of agitating for the Charter, and of setting on foot an *effective* propaganda of social ideas. In compliance with the wishes of my democratic brethren of Newtown, in Wales,[1] I now recure to this subject, and shall

---

1. *Red Republican*, Vol. I No. 6, Notices to Correspondents:

    Newtown, Wales

    I congratulate you on the success of the Red Republican. *Which has attained a circulation in this town far greater than any of the friends had anticipated... perhaps you will excuse the democrats of this town in calling attention to the very able article entitled Chartism in 1850. With the sentiments of the said article we entirely coincide, as far as they go; but we are of the opinion that, inasmuch as the article does not give a definition of social rights, it is so far deficient; and we would earnestly entreat your able correspondent to take the matter up again, and enforce on all section of social reformers, the necessity of defining what they mean by the term 'socialism', and also to urge upon them the necessity of drawing up a plan of social reform, upon which we could all agree. We think Sir, that such a step is absolutely necessary, in order that we may commence an efficient propaganda for democratic and social reform, which shall combine all the scattered elements of progression in one holy and indissoluble band of brotherhood, for the emancipation of the human race from the trinity of humbugs—landlords, fundlords and profitmonger. We are of the opinion*

discuss it as fully as my present limits will allow. In any proposed plan of action, two things must be considered—the *object*, or *ends*, and the *means*. In my opinion, the object of all *real*, that is, of all Social Reformers—and to such alone I speak—*is to improve the social condition of the producers*. The other classes of society, namely, the landlords, and moneylords, being much too well off already. I apprehend therefore, that all questions of Social Reform necessarily relate to the promotion of the physical and moral well being of the veritable People; and that, the desire of extending the social advantages hitherto enjoyed by two privileged castes to the bulk of the nation, hitherto treated as the outcasts of civilization, is the distinguishing characteristic of *real* as opposed to *sham* reformers. *"Every revolution which is not made with a view of profoundly ameliorating the condition of the People, is merely a crime succeeding another crime"*. And in this sentiment of the illustrious Robespierre I heartily agree. Here the question—*Why* we demand such an amelioration? suggests itself. I point to the *Rights of Man. These* are the answer to the question. The Rights of one human being are precisely the same as the Rights of another human being, *in virtue of their common nature*. This natural equality is not affected by the natural *in*equality of physical wants and mental capacity, obtaining between the different individuals belonging to the same species. One man, for example, requires twice as much food as another does, yet the large and the small eater have the same natural *Right* of satisfying their animal wants, and the question of Right has no connection whatever with the question of *capacity*. The same rule holds true in the intellectual world. One man has the mental power of making discoveries in Science, or of assimilating and digesting the contents of whole libraries; another is so stupid that he can scarcely understand the simplest

---

that steps should be taken to bring this subject prominently before the public; therefore we take the liberty of urging upon you to lay it before the leaders, in order that it may be fully discussed previous to the assembly of the next conference. We have long been convinced of the necessity of laying down the groundwork of an agitation for social reform, therefore we wish that a well-digested pamphlet should be drawn up, in the form of the People's Charter, in which the first principles should be laid down and clearly promulgated; and, when once this done, we are confident it will give an immense impetus to our movement. I beg to subscribe myself, on behalf of a few Red Republicans of this town, yours fraternally,
'John Richards'

argument. Yet that is no reason why the latter should be prevented from exercising the Right of satisfying his small intellectual wants; he has the same natural right of doing so that the man of large mental wants has. The law of Equality—which is one of the primitive and inalienable Rights of Man—or rather, it is the all-sustaining groundwork, or substratum, which supports the whole system of human rights and duties—the law of *Equality* is but another term for the law of *Proportion*. *"To every one according to his wants, from every one according to his powers"*, that is the law of the new social arrangements we desire to bring about. The next question which arises is—Of what nature are the arrangements which would express and embody such a law? And here I come to the conflicting theories of the different section of Social Reformers.

Now, it will be necessary to find some common ground upon which they can all meet. I take it for granted that they are all agreed as to the principle of Equality—that they admit that all human beings have a *Right* to the *equal* development and satisfaction of their *unequal* faculties and wants. But what of consequence to me is this *Right*, if society does not give me the *power* of exercising it? I can exercise it only in so far as I have *free access to the instruments of labour, to Land and Capital*.

These are the conditions of my animal existence, and consequently of my mental growth also. Land and Capital, therefore, are national, not individual property. Further, I take it for granted that all sections of Social Reformers are agreed on the necessity of a *radical change* in the existing system of unlimited competition; seeing that, the practical effect of this system has been to plunge the British producers into depths of misery and degradation unsurpassed in the annals of any people. But a radical change can only be effected by substituting the principle of Association for that of Competition, because any measure short of this would be *surface work*, and would leave the root of our social evils untouched. It appears to me, therefore, that the two propositions:

1) The soil and capital are collective property;
2) These instruments of labour being common to All, should be used for the benefit of All, that is, used on the principles of Association and Universal Solidarity;

are propositions resulting from the natural and unalienable Rights of Man, and are common ground upon which all sections of Social Reformers can meet. Many important consequences, into which my limits do not allow me to enter, but which have been fully developed in the works of the Continental Socialists, are derivable from these two fundamental propositions. For example, education is gratuitous and obligatory. Justice is administered gratuitously. The State supports such citizens as are incapable of work, through old age or disease, and this support is not a *charity*, it is a *right*. Private banks are to be abolished, and replaced by a single national bank. Indirect taxation is to be abolished and succeeded by a single direct tax. Usury will be abolished, and replaced by a system of gratuitous national credit. Paper will be substituted for the present metallic currency, and so forth.

If from this consideration of the object of the Social Reformers, I pass onwards to the consideration of the means requisite for its attainment, I find these means are comprised in the two words, *Democratic Organization*, which form the title of the present article. By this organisation, I understand a fusion of all the different sections of Social Reformers, (whether Owenites, National Reform Leaguers, Fraternal Democrats, Red Republicans, Socialists, or Chartists) into one *whole*; having a common fund for the purpose of carrying on a Propaganda of Social Ideas, and having their affairs conducted by a Council, *resident in London*, and elected annually, or oftener, by all members of this organized democratic body. The elements necessary for the execution of this plan exist, though in a scattered state, but it is possible, I think, to combine them. Some of the Welsh brethren agree with me in thinking it is highly necessary to do so forthwith. Because, *united* we may accomplish much; but by *isolated, unconnected* efforts we shall assuredly fail in accomplishing anything except a waste of precious money and still more precious time. I have indicated the ground on which it appears that all *real* reformers can meet, and the principles from which they may start in working together for their common end—*the emancipation of the Wages-Slaves, the abolition of the proletariat.*

So thoroughly am I persuaded of the correctness of what is here advanced, that I call no man a real reformer who does not start from these two fundamental propositions, (the corollaries to the universal Truth of human equality) namely—property is a Social, not an Individual, Right; property ought to be used according to principles which ensure the participation of *all* of its advantages. I call no man a real reformer who does not accept all the consequences which legitimately follow from the above propositions, and who is not prepared to do what he can to ensure the practical and immediate application of these consequences. Anything short of this is *fudge*, because it will leave the question of *Social Misery* just where it was before. As preliminary steps towards this more effective organisation of the democratic interest, I would suggest that a Conference of the Proletarian leaders be held in London forthwith, for the purpose of drawing up a plan or programme of Social Reform upon *Red Republican principles*; that, this plan should be sent to all the various provincial localities where Chartists, Socialists, or Red Republicans exist; and that, they should be required by them, and having the power of making such alterations in the plan as might be deemed advisable. Such a programme once adopted, might be made the basis of the new social propaganda; its various articles would be so many Red Republican texts, from which to preach the Gospel of Socialist-Democracy to the people. I repeat, an extensive Social propaganda is highly necessary; we must not only try to place political power in the hands of the people, we must teach them *how to use it when they have it*. Imagine for a moment, what would be the consequence of Universal Suffrage in the agricultural districts, if the squire and the parson were to continue to lead the agricultural population by the nose!

Another reason, and—as I think an urgent one, for taking steps *immediately* towards combining the scattered elements of democracy into a whole, is the necessity of opposing the designs of the Parliamentary and Financial Reformers. Try these gentlemen by the test of giving the people a share in their own privileges—for example, *in the franchise*, and you will see whether they are the people's friends or not. The close of the [Parliament] session is near, and Messrs. Walmsley, Cobden, Bright and Co., will then commence a crusade, among the working classes, in favour of their own peculiar plans and projects. The Middle-Class leaders have twice led the Proletarians by the nose, viz—in the Reform Bill and the [Anti-Corn Law] League agitations; measures, which by increasing the power of the monied interest—of the mill-owners and shopcrats—have actually made the condition of the producers worse instead of better. These little charter gentry will try it on a third time; and there is no chance of making head against them, unless by the *united* action of the *whole* Ultra-Democratic interest brought to bear on one point. I earnestly beseech the readers of the *Red Republican* to give this matter their most serious consideration; and, if they approve of the line of action indicated above, let them urge it upon the London Social Democracy, either through the medium of this paper, or by direct application to the Executive Council of the National Charter Association. Perhaps, my proletarian brothers, you will think I have spoken dogmatically upon this topic. It is earnestness in the good cause, and no desire of thrusting my private opinions upon others, that has induced me to write as above. I know that the opinions, on practical subjects of one whose training has chiefly been among books and literature, are of little value compared with the opinions of men amongst you, whose education has been continuous battle with the stern realities of life. If, therefore, my judgment of these things be mistaken, let my heartfelt devotion to your cause, plead with you on my behalf.

Proceedings of the Peace-at-any-Price Middle-Class-Humbugs

Red Republican, 21 September 1850

Richer specimens of twaddle than the reports furnished to satiety by all morning and evening newspapers touching the proceedings of the Peace Congress at Frankfurt, it has never been my lot to read.[1] A set of men (supposed to be *sane*) meet together and gravely pass sundry resolutions, all tending to show that, if the various European powers would only consent to adopt a system of international disarmament, and of settling their differences by arbitration, the golden age would descend immediately upon the earth, and the reign of God's saints be at hand. That is, I presume, the *Cotton* Age of the world, and the undisputed reign of profitmongers, railway kings, and other middle-class saints of modern mammon-worship—else we should not find shrewd, practical, Mr Cobden, bringing up the whole force of his *"unadorned eloquence"* in support of such atrocious nonsense. In the third resolution, unanimously adopted by

---

1. In foreign affairs, the Cobden-Bright radicals argued that Free Trade would bring about international and domestic peace. A series of International Congresses of the Friends of Peace took place between 1843 and 1853. The 1850 congress in Frankfurt was attended by British delegates of Liberal, Quaker, Christian Socialist and Unitarian opinion. There were further congresses in London (1851), Manchester (1852) and Edinburgh (1853). The outbreak of the Crimean War of 1853, in which Britain, Turkey, France and Piedmont fought Russia and Bulgaria, put an end to these efforts.

this sapient body, during the first two days of its session, I find the following words: *"That the standing armies with which the governments of Europe menace each other, impose intolerable burdens"*, and so forth, on the unhappy nations obliged to keep these governments and their armies. The resolution then recommends a *"system of international disarmament, without prejudice to such measures as may be considered necessary for the maintenance of the security of the citizens, and the internal tranquility of each state"*.

Fudge! That is the plain English of this unadorned though eloquent sentence. Do the governments of Europe hold their power on any other tenure than that of brute force? If the French government were to disband the *two hundred thousand* soldiers encamped in and about Paris, how long would that disgrace to the very name of a Republic be suffered to exist by an indignant people? If the Hapsburgs were to disband any portion of their colossal standing army, how long would it be before the Hungarians, Italians, Croats, and Poles would reassert their independence, and the Viennese people plant the red flag on the dome of St. Stephen? I presume that the double rows of cannon placed on the ramparts of Vienna, so as to rake the town on the one side, and the suburbs on the other—are intended to overawe *Prussia*, or perhaps *England*; to *"menace each other"* withal! And the gigantic Bastille, now building on the Belvidere, a hill, commanding the most extensive and populous suburbs of the town, suburbs occupied by the *revolutionary Proletariat*—this bastille, bristling with cannon, is doubtless a fortification against the *Turks*, who intend attacking Vienna forthwith! It is evident too, that the Czar and the Prussian Despot have no other fear than that of *foreign* invasion; and that the reason which the English government has large barracks full of soldiers and artillery close beside all the manufacturing towns, and whole armies of constables and semi-military police, at every Chartist demonstration, is the imminent danger we run of an invasion by the Cossacks of the Don. It is not against the people that standing armies are kept. Oh, dear no! The English producers, for instance, are only too well off since we made bread so cheap. Suppose that a starving needlewoman can earn 4½d. by two days hard work at slopshirts, she can get a large brown loaf for that. As to clothing, lodging, washing, fire, candles, food and education for her children, if she have any—she must do without. In fact, she has no business to have any children, Malthus says. Family ties and affections are quite unnecessary luxuries for the wages-slaves; and children are a drug in the labour-market. No, my Proletarian Brothers! Do not believe such stuff as that for a moment, even though all the middle-class leaders, with the eloquent Mr Cobden—*"when unadorned, adorned the most"*[1]—at their head, were to swear to it on their knees. If the bourgeois profitmongering quacks, can make you swallow a *"Morisonian pill"* like *that*, even gilded with *"unadorned eloquence"*[2]—you are donkeys, and deserve to be flogged and overdriven to the end of time. It is a notorious fact that the governments of Europe do not keep standing armies for the purpose of *menacing each other;* but for the purpose of securing their own existence, which is everywhere menaced by the unfortunate people they have so long *mis-*governed; and who cannot be humbugged for ever into remaining quiet under so iniquitous a system of open robbery. *"International disarmament",* consistent with the *"security of the citizens and the internal tranquility of each State"!* That is simply affirming the glaring absurdity, that the security of the *ruling class,* and the continuance of the present system of the using up of one class by another, rests upon any other foundation than that of physical force. It *has* no other foundation. Not one of the continental despots, from Sicily to the Baltic, from the Atlantic to the Black Sea, *durst* dismiss a single soldier, or dismantle a single fortress. And the English government? Let them withdraw their garrisons from the manufacturing districts, and from Ireland—let them disband their constables and dismiss their police spies—and the *"glorious British constitution"* would not survive this suicidal policy a single week. We would have what the perspicuous and luminous author of the Latterday pamphlets [Thomas Carlyle] calls, *"a Chartist parliament and the deluge",* in less than no time.

One of the arguments employed by Mr Cobden, against the present system of standing armies, was taken from a statistical letter by the Baron von Reden,[3] showing that the annual loss to the production of Europe, occasioned by this system, amounted

---

1. Saint Jerome: *"Beauty when unadorned is adorned the most".*
2. The 'Morisonian Pill' was a popular quack medicine called the Vegetable Universal Pill, which was manufactured and sold by the quasi-physician, James Morison (1770–1840).
3. Friedrich Wilhelm von Reden was a pioneering economic statistician employed by the German Zollverein (Customs Union).

Chartist Demonstration

Chartist Procession

to £117,150,000. Truly, a very grievous and distressing reflection for Messrs. Cobden and Co., that the greater part of this money *might now have been in their pockets*, instead of being squandered on useless armies and navies, whose labour cannot be applied to increase the capital of the middle-class profitmongers. That is the meaning of the whole question; the meaning of the *Christian philanthropic and disinterested* outcry about peace, and "*international disarmament*", made by these peace-at-any-price middle class humbugs. The question is a middle class question; and concerns the Proletarians, only insofar as it exposes the selfishness and absurdity of their pretended Middle Class friends, who leave no stone unturned to gull the producers into the *belief, that the interest of labour and capital are the same. But they are not the same; they are directly contrary*, and can never cease to be so, in the system of *Wages-labour*. A shocking loss of Messrs. Cobden, and Co., that of £117,150,000, on the production of Europe! But the proletarians need not care how much is lost on the production of Europe, for devil a penny of that money would ever have found its way to them. But the extension of trade! The increase of production, and the consequent demand for labour!

From 1839 to 1849 our trade was greatly extended, our production was greatly increased, our country advanced in wealth—did the improvement in the condition of our working population, our *wealth-producers*, keep pace with this development of our resources, this increase of National wealth? Are *poor-rates* and *taxation* less now than they were ten years ago? It is notorious that they are nothing of the kind—and all the lamentations of these hypocritical humbugs at Frankfurt about the evils of war establishments during peace, are merely the expressions of their selfish regret at so much hard cash having been diverted from its legitimate channel—namely, the pockets of middle class blood-sucking profit-mongers. The commercial history of the last ten years, proves, that the condition of the producing class has become positively worse, with every successive development of the modern system of production and distribution. It proves, that when capital flourishes, labour perishes; it proves, that the interests of the employer and the employed are diametrically opposite interests, and that one can prosper only by using up the other. The increase in poor-rates during the last ten years, is alone sufficient to show that the condition of the wealth-producers, the veritable people, has become worse—that misery and starvation are more busily at work than ever. Do not, therefore, believe any middle class humbug, who tells you that a *decrease* in any branch of the public expenditure, for example, in *"the expense of our army and navy"*, would be accompanied by a proportionate *increase* of comfort to *you*; that *your wages* would thereby be increased. Every increase of national wealth, either by saving or by directly producing, goes to increase capital, not wages—goes into the pockets of the middle-class, not into those of the Proletariat. The proof of this is evident enough. Is not the condition of the working class infinitely worse *now* than it was forty or fifty years ago? Yet look at the difference between the capital and the productive power of to-day as compared with those possessed by us half a century ago. The means of comfort and happiness for all have greatly increased, but they are managed on so nefarious a system, that *nine-tenths* of the population of every civilised country are miserable, starving wretches; while the *remaining tenth* monopolises everything that can make life either desirable or endurable. That state of things, is Society arranged on middle class principles. Do you think the principles which produce such practical effects, are good, and just, and true principles? I think they are *false*, and *unjust*, and *anti-Christian*, and altogether *damnable* principles. But be they what they may, they will never be changed as long as *political power* remains in the hands of the middle class.

Mr Cobden then remarks that *"you cannot have freedom and self-government unless you have also a spirit of order and tranquility pervading all classes"*. A contradiction in terms. As long as Society is divided in *classes*, so long will the social system be founded on the distinction of a ruling class and a subordinate class—the oppressed and the oppressor. Now, if there be *"a spirit of order and tranquility pervading"* the oppressed class, it must be a remarkable stupid class indeed. But as far as my researches have extended into universal history, I have never yet found an instance of an oppressed class being what their rulers would call *"orderly and tranquil"*. Had they been contented with their sad fate, *they would have deserved it*. No. The Slaves of all ages, the Helots of Sparta, the Roman bondmen, the serfs of the middle ages, the Negro and Proletarian Slaves of modern times, have amply and energetically protested against that atrocious system of one class using up another; a system which can only be enforced and continued in any country by the unlimited use of the whip and the bayonet. There is no danger of a European war? That is not the danger: the danger everywhere is financial. *"How can we get more money?"* is the outcry. But a European war is the necessary consequence of this financial danger. Not a war between the governments of Europe, though they incessantly *"menace each other"*; *but a war of the European nations against their representative Governments*, which I grieve to say is quite inevitable, and likewise near at hand—in spite of the probable injury to the sale of Manchester cottons, and the virtuous indignation of Messrs. Cobden, and Co. The present system of physical force repression must naturally come to an end sooner or later. The finale will be hastened, in every country, by the pressure of a large national debt, and a grinding system of indirect taxation; in a word, by *"financial danger"*.

Mr Cobden concludes his oration by an *"appeal to Governments and kings, as well as tax-payers and the people, to keep a cause that will bless and benefit them all"*. This is assuming that the interest of governments and kings *"is the same as tax-payers and the people, to keep a cause that will bless and benefit them all"*. This is assuming that the interest of governments and kings *is the same* as the interest of the subjects whom they scourge, imprison, and slaughter, to prevent being hurled from the thrones they have too long occupied. The *"governments and kings"* of whom he speaks, are not such fools as he takes them to be. Disband their armies, quotha! It is asking a drowning man to cast away his plank. I agree with Mr Cobden that *"the possession of enormous military power will not prevent revolutions"*. But what cannot be *prevented* may be *postponed*. That is precisely what *"governments and kings"* are now doing. Postponing the revolution by any and every means; and thereby prolonging their own lives. But the longer the next outbreak of the European revolution is delayed, the more terrible will it be when it does come. God grant it may be the last.

The 'Morning Post' and the Woman Flogger

Red Republican, 21 September 1850

I have been informed that the *Morning Post* has displayed great sympathy for the sad case of His Excellency the Herr Baron von Haynau.[1] A poor old man, nearly seventy years of age, is set upon and misused by a crowd of some hundred individuals! What a disgrace to England! And so forth, through infinite variations of lamentation and woe. I say I was *informed* of this; for I never read the *Morning Post*, having too much respect for my sanity to risk its loss, by rashly encountering unfathomable floods of twaddle. I believe the first civil engineer on record is Milton's Devil, who threw an elegant suspension bridge over Chaos, having first explored it by a new mode of locomotion, *"half wading, half flying"*,—but the devil himself would stand aghast at the Chaos of fudge heaped together in the columns of the *Morning Post*. This paper having given one side of the picture, let us look a moment at the other side. A hoary-headed old ruffian orders *women to be stripped naked and flogged till nearly dead, by a set of savage soldiers*. And these executors of his lawless will were not half so brutal as this *"noble and knightly gentleman"*—this Austrian

---

1. When in July 1850, Haynau, during a semi-official London visit, called at the Barclays and Perkins brewery on Bankside, word got around the Chartist-supporting workers that the 'Butcher Haynau' was in their midst. The workers set upon him and attempted to drown him in a barrel of beer; he narrowly escaped with his life and had to be rescued by a squad of constables.

commander-in-chief, who, in some instances, personally superintended the civilized and refined operation; and, in all instances, would have tried and condemned anyone venturing to remonstrate against such barbarity—by a drumhead court martial. Of what terrible, revolting crime had these unhappy women been guilty? They had aided their husbands, their fathers, their brothers, in the Hungarian and Italian insurrections. They had aided those to whom they were bound by every natural and *legal* tie.

They had committed the horrible crime of taking for granted, that those whom they had been taught from their infancy to respect, whom they had been sedulously instructed to *reverence* and *obey*, on whose judgment they had been accustomed to rely— were better judges than they, as to the propriety of shaking off the Austrian despot's yoke. For this horrible crime against "*family property, and order*"—these women were stripped naked and flogged, by order of the infamous, unmanly *coward*—his excellency the Herr Baron von Haynau. Do you dare to justify such brutality, editor though you be of the... Morning Post, court lackey, and aristocratic toady, generally? Then you are about as great a brute as the wretch whose abominations you attempt to excuse. You are a fit eulogist and apologist for a woman-flogger. Had I been present, when those brave proletarians gave this ruffian his deserts, I should certainly have dissuaded "*the mob from using violence*", that is, from actually laying *hands on him*. I would have said, brothers, your hands are hardened and blackened with honourable toil. Do not pollute them by *touching* that beast. Take mops and brooms, sweep him out as you do other kinds of dirt. Like to like. Filth to filth. Haynau to the common sewer!—I do not wonder at the apology of the *Morning Post* having been echoed by the *Times*, the *Globe* the *Chronicle*, and other papers—the organs of the "*middle and higher classes*",—and that Baron Rothschild should be the friend of such a ruffian as this Austrian Woman-flogger.[1] For the supremacy of the ruling class must be kept up at any and every price; and this stockbrokering son of Israel found his financial operations a good deal hindered, his profits a good deal diminished, and the safety of his loans a good deal endangered, by the late disturbances in the Austrian empire.

---

1. Sir Anthony Nathan de Rothschild (1810–1876), financier and hereditary baron of the Austrian Empire, was made the 1st Baronet de Rothschild in 1847 by Queen Victoria.

Perish the human race! Let Justice be a fiction, and Fraternity a delusion! What matter, if the coronetted Shylocks of the Stock-exchange thrive? *"Oh my daughter and my ducats! My ducats and my daughter!"*[1]

Some of the Austro-Russian press gang have expressed their surprise that low people, like draymen, coal-heavers, and so forth, should understand anything about continental affairs. Always the old story. Do they think, then, that the world is standing still, that even the 'lowest class' of English Proletarians are now so ignorant as the besotted mob who were hounded on by the Tories to burn down Priestley's house and to persecute every Reformer in *"the good old times"*.[2] The besotted fools our fathers who believed whatever the landlord and the parson chose to tell them! Who proclaimed the important fact to an admiring universe, that *"one Englishman could lick ten Frenchmen"*—*"Britons never shall be slaves"*, and the like—even when Pitt was saddling them and their children with a debt contracted for the purpose of stifling the germs of Liberty through Europe, and they were the veriest slaves of a ruling class, of a vile oligarchy!—as much slaves as the Helots of Lacedemon, or the serfs of the middle ages. Thank God! that time has gone by. And the events of the last two years have done more to enlighten the people on their true position, than centuries of preaching. Universal History is the best *"enlightener"*. Its lessons, you see, have reached even coalheavers, draymen, and costermongers—about whose *humanity*, the readers of an enlightened press *"conducted by able editors"*, have entertained doubts. Yet they are men, and *thinking* men too. I honour them, and congratulate them, from the bottom of my heart.

---

1. Shakespeare, *Merchant of Venice*, Scene VIII.
2. Joseph Priestley (1733–1804) was a Unitarian clergyman, natural philosopher and chemist (credited with the discovery of oxygen). His outspoken support of the French Revolution aroused the Church and King Mobs, who torched his Birmingham house. To escape government persecution he went into exile in Pennsylvania.

The Democratic and Social Republic

Red Republican, 12 October 1850

We, who rally around the Red Flag, are reproached with entertaining the nefarious design of completely destroying the existing order of things: with the desire of totally abolishing the present system of society—for the purpose, it is said, of putting some fantastic dream, some wild Utopia of our own, in the place of long established and venerable institutions. Truly a terrible accusation, this! No wonder that bankers, cotton spinners, landowners, and other 'practical' persons, should sneer at such a design; or that, *"promising young men"* should look down upon us with contempt from Treasury benches, and other official heights; or that *"superior women"*, educated according to the recipes of Mrs Ellis for *"making admirable wives and mothers"*, should not be able to conceal their disgust.[1]

"What! You, who have neither wealth nor learning, nor position in society, who are a low rabble without a single respectable man among you—pretend to accomplish a social revolution in this country!" It is true we intend doing this very thing. And what our adversaries consider as a reproach—we consider the greatest praise that could be given us. We are low people certainly; disreputable vag-

---

1. Sarah Stickney Ellis (1799–1872), a Quaker turned Congregationalist, wrote numerous books on the religious and domestic duties of middle-class women and girls. She established a school at Rawdon House in Hertfordshire for the *"moral training, the formation of character, and in some degree the domestic duties of young ladies"*.

abonds without doubt. In ancient times we were accounted *"the enemies of the human race"*, accused of setting fire to Rome, and of doing other things deserving the severest punishments.

I am happy to say that we still retain our old reputation: we are now the *"enemies of family, property, and order"*, and have not failed to follow the laudable example of our precursors in Roman times, by making ourselves obnoxious to *"principalities and powers, to spiritual wickedness in high places"*. We are chiefly proletarians. I find it fitting that the work of realising the democratic idea should be entrusted to working men; seeing that this idea first dawned upon the mind of a working man, who meditated on it for thirty years, and then threw aside his joiner's tools, to go forth and teach it to other proletarians, *"fishermen, publicans, sinners"*,—in fact a low rabble with not a single respectable man among them. Yet even in England, this shopkeeping country of middle-class respectability there are a few of us belonging to the 'better sort' who have repudiated all claim to be considered respectable,[1] because for them the words Justice and Love are not mere empty sounds without a meaning; because they say—like Antigone in Sophocles—the laws of God are not of today, nor of yesterday, they exist from all eternity.[2]

---

1. Macfarlane's self-recognition as being one of *"few of us belonging to the 'better sort'"* echoes the lines of the Communist Manifesto which celebrate the fact that: *"a part of the bourgeoisie is joining the proletariat, and particularly a part of bourgeois ideologists, or middle-class thinkers who have attained a theoretical knowledge of the whole historical movement"*.

2. In this remarkable unfurling of the Red Flag as the enactment of 'laws of God' which 'exist from all eternity', Macfarlane seems to be influenced by Hegel's analysis of Sophocles' *Antigone*. In the battle for control of the city of Thebes, Antigone's two brothers, Polyneices and Eteocles are killed fighting each other. Their uncle, Creon, inherits the throne and decrees that, whilst Eteocles should be buried with full honours, the rebel Polyneices should be left outside the walls of the city to be eaten by the birds. Antigone refuses to accept this and, despite threats from Creon that he will bury her alive, she buries Polyneices according to the tribal religion and she wins Creon's son Haemon over to her side. The conflict ends in disaster for all concerned. Hegel sees the dramatic clash in as between two irreconcilable principles: the human law of the State—which is cruel, but nonetheless, historically 'progressive'—and divine (family) law. As quoted by Hegel and echoed by Macfarlane, Antigone says of this

Yes, we will change the existing state of things. For we are heartily tired of a society founded upon constitutional lies, and the basest selfishness. We are sick to death of hearing that the jails and hulks are recruited from the starving ranks of labour; that nine-tenths of the women workers in the streets are driven to that fearful life by hunger; that hundreds upon hundreds of men, toiling day and night at carpentry and other trades, can make about 5s. a week for the support of themselves and families; that the workhouses are filled to overflowing with *able-bodied* men; that human beings die every now and then of hunger in the streets, without any special notice being taken of so common an occurrence; that thousand upon thousands of men and women have no other home than filthy dens and cellars, where a rich man would not put his pigs; that thirty thousand women, *in London alone*, are starving at shirtmaking; that men work 18 hours a day, baking bread in hot, unhealthy places, for a pittance hardly sufficient to keep soul and body together.

We are disgusted at seeing priests of Baal, professing the religion of fraternity, standing up in pulpits and audaciously blaspheming this holy idea. Professing it with their lips, reading it aloud at altars, while their whole lives give it the lie; while they defend a social system, which is based on the principle that one man, or one class, has a right to enslave and trample on another.

We have heard long enough of the misery pervading distracted, unhappy Ireland—where the 'rights of property' are so well protected that whole families are almost daily turned out to starve on the roadside, at the will and pleasure of the landowning class. We are ashamed of living in comparative comfort when so many of our fellow creatures are dragging out so miserable an existence.

We feel humiliated and pained when a beggar stretches out his hand to us for 'charity'—that insult and indignity offered to human nature; that word invented by tyrants and slavedrivers—an infamous word, which we desire to see erased from the language of every civilised people.

---

divine law: *"Not now, indeed, nor yesterday, but for aye / It lives, and no man knows what time it came."*
Antigone, as the supposedly less 'civilized' of the two colliding forces gains, in Hegel's words, a *"self-conscious actual universality"* in standing up to the state, and standing out from those in her community *"who think as I do but dare not speak".* Hegel, Phenomenology of Spirit, para 448.

Surely a social system which produces such fruits as these, cannot be a good one. We believe, that unless God be a fiction, justice a chimera, truth a lie—it is possible to find social arrangements in virtue of which all the inhabitants of a given country could obtain a fair share, not only of the necessities, but of the comforts and luxuries of life—*in exchange for the honest labour of their own hands*. In other word, we believe it as quite possible to enact laws whereby the rights of every man might be secured, without encroaching on the rights of his fellows. That is our dream, that is our Utopia; it is the democratic and social republic. We are the friends of the poor, the suffering, the oppressed—a sufficient reason for being hated by the dominant classes, and calumniated by the base press-gang which supports them. A mad dog is joke compared to a Red Republican. We consider that the duty of working and the right to a comfortable existence resulting from that duty, are common to all mankind—the primeval duty and right inherent in human nature. But he who does not fulfil this duty has no just claim to its reward; he is a thief who lives by robbing his fellows. We recognise the justice of that wise saying of an ancient leader amongst us, "*He that does not work, neither shall he eat*".

To prevent any person from living on the labour of others—to prevent any one from being used as a wage slave; to put an end at once and for ever to this iniquitous system of class-supremacy and class legislation, which is simply the sway of a horde of bandits and murderers, veiled under legal and constitutional forms—to abolish the distinction existing between tax-payers and tax-eaters, between producers and non-producers, is the aim of the Democratic and Social Republic. We call by this name, a system of social arrangements based on the principles—Equality, Liberty, Fraternity. A social system which recognises the equal rights of every rational human being—which ignores frivolous and superficial distinctions, as of rank, colour, sex, country and the like. Just laws which say—one man shall not be allowed to starve while another has more food than he can eat; one woman shall not be allowed to die by inches, making slopshirts at 2d. a piece, while another, whose brow is encircled by a crown or coronet, does not know what it is to have a caprice ungratified; one child shall not be left to grow up in dirt and rags and brutalising ignorance, in the filthy lanes and gutters of the manufacturing towns, while another is clothed in purple and fine linen—pampered and spoiled by a host of obsequious servants, tutors and governesses. Do you now understand now the meaning of the words, Democracy and Social Republic? They are the embodiment of that dying prayer of our first martyr, *"That all may be one, even as we are one"*.[1] They re-echo the dying prophecy of another of our glorious martyrs, the Saxon Blum, who gave his breast to the bullets of the Austrian assassin, rather than renounce his religion of fraternity.[2] You ask, my Proletarian brothers—in what do these social arrangements consist? And in what manner can they be realised? The first step towards their realisation is the enactment of the Charter. I affirm that no really democratic arrangement of society is possible, except on the really democratic foundation of Universal Suffrage. Anything short of this is fudge. If you leave political power in the hands of any *part* of a nation, instead of extending its possession to the *whole* people, you immediately have the distinction of a ruling and a subordinate class; of one class which makes laws—of course for its own advantage, and another, which must obey those class laws, whether it find them just or not. On one hand, you have the master, on the other, the slave. Do not, therefore, be humbugged by that set of political quacks who now offer you *"Household Suffrage"*—a *"moderate extension of the Suffrage"*, as a middle-class nostrum to cure your social miseries. That is a cheat, like all Middle class measures, like the Reform Bill and Free Trade. Has that Morissonian pill of Messrs. Cobden, Bright, etc., delivered us from pauperism? From the fear of over-production, glut in the market, commercial crisis, short time, reduction of wages, want of work?—pleasant little peculiarities of the Middle-class system of production and distribution, which simply mean, *for the Working Class*, starvation, ruin and death? No—it has done nothing of the kind. Whenever that set of brazen-faced charlatans come again before you with their stereotype cry, *"listen to us, follow our guidance, and all will go well"*, do not listen to them. You have done so twice too often already. Hiss them off the platforms whence they delight to spout *"unadorned eloquence and thoroughly liberal speeches"* as hypocrites and impostors; if they dare any longer to call themselves your

---

1. John 17:22

2. Robert Blum (1807–1848) was a radical German democrat and parliamentarian. Present in Vienna during the suppression of the 1848 Revolution, Blum was illegally arrested by the military authorities and executed by firing squad.

friends, while refusing you the franchise in order to use you up as wages slaves.

The Charter once enacted, the delegates of the people will form the government. The first thing to be done then will be to pass a series of measures calculated to serve as a means of transition from the old to the new epoch. For example; the land will be declared national property. Agricultural colonies will be founded in every country parish. A great proportion of the population will be at once withdrawn from the crowded streets of our manufacturing towns, to form industrial armies organised for agricultural purposes, under competent chiefs, appointed at first by the state; afterwards to be elected by members of each colony. Then the houses left vacant in the towns, by this means, will be pulled down; and wide, clean, well-ventilated streets will take the place of the present filthy holes and corners, the fitting habitus for disease and crime. The state will constitute itself the national banker, fire and life insurer, railway and canal, gas and waterworks proprietor. From these sources, the enormous profits formerly made by private companies being reduced to a very moderate rate—a large public revenue will be derived and applied at once to the organisation of labour; the labour-budget being the only budget under the new *regime*. Indirect taxation will be abolished: a temporary, direct, and progressive poll-tax will be substituted for the purpose of defraying the most pressing public expenses, such as the administration of justice and a national system of secular education, both gratuitous. Simultaneous with the organisation of agricultural labour will be the organisation of commerce and manufactures, on the principle of association and solidarity. The property of state churches will be confiscated for the benefit of the labour budget. The state, engaging at the same time, to give such of the priests as cannot find congregations willing to pay them on the voluntary principle, a sum sufficient to supply them with the necessities of life, until they can be absorbed in the ranks of labour. Let them learn trades, like Paul of Tarsus, who *"worked with his own hands as a tentmaker"*, who did not merely preach and prate about the text, *"he that will not work, neither shall he eat"*, but acted up to his own maxim as an honest man.

What a hideous cry outcry of robbery, sacrilege etc., etc. would be raised by these idolatrous Mammon-worshippers, these fat priests of ball—bishops, deans, cannons, rectors, vicars, whose

The Democratic and Social Republic

name is legion—when they saw themselves reduced to this state of Apostolic simplicity! But the state might justly ask, "*Of what do you complain, good people?*" You threaten us with the consequences of this sacrilegious act. Well, then we shall act upon the text which says, "*With whatever measure you mete unto others, shall it be meted unto you again*". We shall treat you precisely as you treated the Catholics in the 16th century. We will kick you out of that property without giving you any means of subsistence at all. Thank your stars that you get leave to rave and rage and grumble as much as you like, without being burned alive at Smithfield, or set in the pillory with your nose slit and your ears cut off; these things being, as you know, Church of England receipts to cure Roman Catholic grumblers, much used in the time of two enlightened Protestant sovereigns, Elizabeth and James.

These, and similar measures, my Proletarian brothers, will constitute the means of transition from the present state of things into quite another state, which we call the Democratic and Social Republic. From the above slight sketch you will see that the stereotyped cry of the reactionists, the leave-alone, the leave-to-suffer, leave-to-die, gentry—is absurd. We do not wish to make the rich man poor; to deprive the capitalists of his unjust gains. Let them, in God's name, keep what they have already got, under a vicious system which has victimised us all nearly alike. Victimised the Proletarian, by ignorance, physical suffering—and the degradation consequent upon this neglect of both soul and body. Victimised the capitalist, by blunting the moral sentiment in him to such a degree, that he has become incapable of distinguishing between right and wrong, between truth and falsehood; he has renounced reason, the birthright of humanity, and is content to be—not a man, but a cotton-spinner. He has no soul, only a bank bill. His moral law, ten commandments, thirty-nine articles, and confession of faith, are all compromised in the words, cash payment. He is a greater brute than the miserable, ragged, drunken, ignorant serf, that he uses up in his mills and factories. But one thing is quite certain, when political power is once fairly placed in hands by means of the Charter, we will use that power to prevent any further accumulations of capital in the hands of *individuals*. For the principle which is at the bottom of our system is, that property is a *Social* right, not an *Individual* one.

If you acknowledge the validity of the principles Equality, Liberty, Fraternity, by what process of logic will you grant the right of access to the instruments of labour, namely—land and capital, to one individual and deny it to another? We will make no *"half-revolution"*. We will have a *social* revolution, or none at *all*. Justice for all, or justice for none. Political power is the means—the reign of Equality, Liberty, Fraternity, is the end. Let us work for the possession of this power, then, for the enactment of the Charter, with courage and hope for our companions. For the Democratic and Social Republic, the El Dorado, or golden age of the world, does not lie in the past, it lies in the future history of humanity.

Labour *versus* Capital: Two Chapters on Humbug

Red Republican, **2 & 9 November 1850**

Chapter one

Brother Proletarians—So many kinds of fallacies and fudge are being at present diligently propagated regarding the above subjects, that, were I to direct your attention towards the tenth part of them, I might fill the columns of the *Red Republican* every week. At present, therefore, I shall discuss only three kinds of 'respectable' fudge, which have been specially brought under my notice of late. One set of Humbug-Manufacturers boldly deny the existence of antagonistic classes. In England— 'this highly respectable firm', is represented by rose-coloured political sentimentalists, of the Boz school, and by the pious patrons of congresses for the promotion of universal peace. In France, the sapient persons who live in the pleasing delusion that there is no such thing as antagonistic classes, with diametrically opposite interests, are represented by the stump-orator and Cockney litterateur, *par excellence*, M. de Lamartine.[1] During a recent visit to England, this 'Justice Midas'[2] of the conservative bourgeoisie,

---

1. Alphonse de Lamartine (1790–1869) was a French historian, poet and liberal republican who served as Minister of Foreign Affairs from February to May 1848 in the Revolutionary government.
2. A popular burletta, *Midas*, by the Irish playwright, Kane O'Hara (1714–82) has the following lines: **Midas:** *What the Devil's here to do, Ye loggerheads and gypsies? / Sirrah you, and hussy you / And each of*

made the astounding discovery that John Bull lives in an earthly paradise, where no apprehensions need be entertained of any collision between the different classes composing society. During the last twenty years, according to M. de Lamartine, England has made immense progress,

> not only in population, in riches, industry, navigation, railroads, extent, edifices, embellishments, and the health of the capital, but also, and more especially, in charitable institutions for the people, and in associations of real religious, conservative, and fraternal socialism between classes, to prevent explosions, by the evaporation of the causes which produce them—to stifle the murmurs from below, by incalculable benefits from above—and to close the mouths of the people, not by the brutalities of the police, but by the arm of public virtue.

M. de Lamartine eulogises the charity, the prudence, the public virtue of 'that intelligent aristocracy', viz—the English; gives a sketch of England as it appeared to him in 1822, 1830, and, lastly, in 1850. He states that, in 1830,

> it was the misery of the English and Irish Proletarians that frightened observers. Ireland was literally dying of inanition. The manufacturing districts of the three kingdoms having produced more than the world could consume, during the fifteen years of peace, left an overflow of manufactures—the masses were emaciated, vitiated in body and mind—vitiated by their hatred against the class of society who possess. The manufacturers had dismissed armies of workmen without bread. These black columns were to be seen with their mad-coloured jackets, dotting the avenues and streets of London, like columns of insects, whose nests had been upset. The vices and brutishness of these masses of Proletarians, degraded by hunger and ignorance—their alternate poverty and debaucheries—their promiscuousness of ages, of sexes, of dens of foetid straw—their bedding in cellars and garrets—their hideous clamours, to be met with at certain hours in the morning, in certain lanes of the unclean districts of London—when those human vermin emerged into the light of the sun with howling, groaning, or laughter that was really satanic, it would have made the masses

---

you tipsy is; / But I'll as sure pull down your pride as, / A gun, or as I'm justice Midas / **Chorus:** Oh tremendous justice Midas! / Who shall oppose wise justice Midas?"

of free creatures envy the fate of the black slaves of our colonies... Social war was visible there, with all its horrors and its furies— everybody saw it, and I myself forboded it, like everybody else.

Such was the aspect of things in general twenty years ago. M. de Lamartine revisits us now and finds everything changed for the better; I presume, through the 'incalculable benefits from above', so liberally showered down by 'that intelligent aristocracy'. In the streets of London he finds an amazing difference:

the ignoble lanes, with their suspicious taverns, where the population of drunken sailors, huddled together, like savages, in dregs and dust, have been demolished... those streets are now as well cleaned from filth, drunkenness, and obscenity, as the other streets and suburbs of the city—one can pass through them without pity and disgust; one feels in them the vigilance of public morality, and the presence of a police which, if it cannot destroy vice, can at all events keep it at a distance from the eyes of the passer-by... If you read the journals, these safety-valves of public opinion, you must remain struck with the extreme mildness of men's minds and hearts, with the temperance of ideas, the moderation of what is desired, the prudence of the liberal opposition, the tenderness evinced towards a conciliation of all classes... the readiness of all to co-operate, each according his means and disposition, in advancing the general good—the employment, comfort, instruction, and morality of the people... One feels that this people can live, last, prosper, and improve, for a long time in this way.

Yet, "*two classes of men, whom nothing ever satisfies, the demagogues and extreme aristocrats*", are exempted from this happy state of middle-class bliss and security! But a few "*clubs of Chartists and of diplomatists*" cannot disturb the profound calm which prevails in a country ruled by an 'intelligent aristocracy'—which dispenses 'incalculable benefits from above', through the medium of a glorious constitution, and a set of time-honoured, venerable institutions. Unique specimens of middle-class twaddle, these extracts, are they not? I think they ought to be worked in elaborate tentstitch, framed, glazed, and sent to the Exhibition of '51—that great repository of middle-class humbug.

I will not insult your judgment, my Proletarian brothers, by commenting at much length on such stuff as the above. We, who suffer from the tyranny of the money-grubbers—we, who must bear the misery inflicted on the enslaved classes by an odious, unjust system of society—know too well already what amount of faith can be placed in such descriptions of middle-class moderation and mildness—of prosperity *for us*, under class-supremacy and class-legislation. The *charity* of an 'intelligent aristocracy!' But the charity of the aristocrat is an abominable insult to the plebeian. Let us fling them back their 'charity'. We do not want it. What we want is *justice*, not charity—a *right*, not an 'incalculable benefit from above'. As children of the same Father, we demand that share in the advantages of civilisation of which we have been scandalously robbed; we demand our *birthright* as human beings—as rational, moral agents. That which we hold directly from God, in virtue of our humanity, we will not degrade ourselves by receiving as a *favour*, a 'charity', at the hands of any human being, still less at those of rascally aristocrats, whether landed or financial. 'Incalculable benefits from above!' Are the aristocrats *gods*, that they assume the position of dispensing 'incalculable benefits' to others? I have yet to learn that any merely *human* being can confer benefits, calculable or incalculable, upon his fellows. He simply performs his *duty*, or he does not perform it. His duty is to refrain from all interference with the *rights* of others; it is to aid them in enforcing these rights, if need be; in a word, 'to do unto others as ye would that others should do unto you'. Accept this sublime moral law—the interpretation of the words, Equality, Liberty, Fraternity—and there could be, henceforth and for ever, no mention between man and man of such things as 'charity, favours, obligations, benefits'. These are vile words, the invention of tyrants, and ought to be blotted for ever from the language of freemen. I suppose we must reckon the recent Whig refusals to extend the Suffrage, to repeal the knowledge tax, to permit the secular education of the people, among the 'incalculable benefits' lately conferred upon us by an 'intelligent aristocracy'. From *such* benefits, good Lord deliver us! Yet, I think, they are not *incalculable*. We know pretty well how much they are worth. 'Ireland was literally dying of inanition in 1830', and in 1850, of course, the Irish proletarians are well-fed and contented; only they are flying by thousands from that unhappy country to avoid being starved to death; and even a correspondent of the Times admits that, in some of the southern districts, 'one would be puzzled to say where the next generation of men were to come from!'

In 1830, 'the masses were vitiated by their hatred of the class of society who possess'. And if this silly cockney disciple of the French reactionist party really knew anything of the sentiments prevalent amongst the working-men of England, he would know that their hatred of 'the deleterious middle class'—of those 'who possess' by robbing others—is as rife now as it was in 1830, God be thanked! God be thanked that the human mind has not stood still during the last twenty years, else were our hopes of salvation faint indeed. M. de Lamartine's congratulations upon the 'vigilance of public morality' are rather premature. In 1845, I was informed, by an eminent physician in London, that the number of *there* was about 80,000. In 1850, I have been told the number is about 100,000; to which increase in the victims of a class-legislation, the *cheap Bibles*, patronised by the saints of moral England, have largely contributed.[1] As to the other topics discussed by M. de Lamartine, I think recent events furnish an amusing enough commentary thereon. The 'extreme mildness and moderation of the journals' was lately shown in their defence of the Austrian assassin and woman-flogger, in their angry vituperation of the brave Proletarians, who drove him forth like a wild beast, as he is. 'The tenderness evinced towards a conciliation of classes' is peculiarly evinced in the speeches of Mr Bright and others, the organs of the mill-owning, manufacturing portion of the middle-class. The anxiety of these gentlemen for 'the general good, for the comfort, instruction, and morality of the people' is shown by their opposition to the Ten Hours' Bill, to all inquiries into the state of the labouring poor, etc., etc. Doubtless, too, it is for the 'general good' of the working-class that they are to be delivered, bound hand and foot, into the power of merciless despots like the Gooches and Faggs[2]—like the factory lords, 'who grind the faces of the poor', through the infamous relay system—else we should not see 'the safety-valves of public opinion'—newspapers, that is—written for the so-called upper and middle classes—up-

---

1. Macfarlane's readers would have known of a widely-reported meeting held in London in 1850 to protest the conditions of female book-binders employed by the Bible Society. It was said that the women were so badly paid for their labour that many of them had to resort to prostitution to make ends meet.
2. Sir Daniel Gooch (1816–1889) was the Great Western 'Railway King', later Conservative MP. Fagg, whoever he was, appears to have been forgotten.

holding, *without one exception*, the capitalist-tyrants in their iniquitous war against labour.

Chapter two: labour *versus* capital

Another set of Humbug Manufacturers do not deny the existence of antagonistic classes. They do not wilfully shut their eyes to what is passing around them. They acknowledge the existence of hideous evils—for example, that since 1810 our population has increased 60 per cent, while crime has increased at the rate of 420 per cent during the same period; that the total amount of poor rates collected in England and Wales since 1839, is fifty millions sterling; that in England about one in twelve of the population—in Scotland, one in nine—in Ireland, one in eight—are *paupers*, as shown by the poor-law returns for 1848; but the remedy proposed by this set of quacks is emigration. Every sane man knows that the same causes invariably produce the same effects. If you wish, therefore, to get rid of such effects as these facts I have quoted, you must make a thorough change in the vicious, unnatural system, which has produced them. You must arrange society upon totally different principles. Yet now, all would go well, we are told, if a certain number of our 'surplus population' were drafted off every year. It appears that this surplus amounts to about four millions in ten years. Were it possible to draft off this number during the next ten years, and so arrange matters that the population of the United Kingdom should be, in 1860, pretty much the same as it is in 1850, I cannot see that the condition of the *Proletarian* class would be in the least improved by it. Take the following account of the present condition of the people in Dorsetshire, a county of which the squirearchy and state clergy hold undisputed possession, where the labourer vegetates in peace, far removed from the contaminating influences of Chartism, Socialism, and other kinds of 'awful infidelity'. This extract is from the *Times*, quoted by a Mr Christopher, in his recent work on Emigration—"*Measured by the infallible test of crime, Dorsetshire is fast sinking into a slough of wretchedness which threatens the peace and morality of the kingdom at large... It is no light affair, that a rural county, the abode of an ancient and respectable aristocracy, somewhat removed from the popular influences of the age, with a population of 175,043 by the last census, should produce in four years nearly 3,000 convictions, being at the rate of one conviction in that pe-*

riod for every sixty persons, or every twelve households". It is precisely because this county is removed from the popular influences of the age, and its population left to grow up in brutal ignorance, by 'an ancient', but very disrespectful aristocracy, in order to be used up, by the latter, as beasts of burden, that crime is so rife there. And, provided the population of Dorsetshire were to be kept stationary for the next ten years, by drafting off the surplus, yet the condition of the people would not be ameliorated thereby; for the *causes* which have produced this misery and its attendant crime, would still remain at work as busily as ever—and the remedy for the social cancer which is devouring us, is emigration! European society, with its vicious organisation of labour, is to be transported *en masse* to new countries, and the world will be saved. An experiment which has signally failed in America. A country not half peopled as yet. A country with an unlimited supply of fertile territory in the far West, and in the newly-annexed states. Yet, the middle-class system of production and distribution, which has occasioned evils, now fast becoming intolerable, in the old world, is making itself felt in the new one also. The agrarian reformers there, however, are taking the bull by the horns—they are boldly grappling the land question.[1] Emigration is among those petty, peddling, hole-and-corner, surface reforms—skin-deep remedies for a vital disease—at present propounded by political and social quacks, who either cannot or *will* not see, that *a radical change in existing social arrangements* is the one thing needful, in order to give the Proletarian a chance for his life. During the last few years, for example, thousands upon thousands of Irish Proletarians, have fled from their country, while those who remained have been literally *decimated* by hunger and disease. Despite this 'removal of the surplus population', the condition of the Irish peasant has not improved. It will never do so under the present system; never, until there has been a *social revolution* in that country.

The third kind of 'respectable' fudge lately brought under my notice, is perhaps, the most disgusting kind extant. It may be called the pious, or Evangelical sort of fudge. It is patronised chiefly by Lord Ashley and his gang of hypocritical, Anti-Sab-

---

[1] The National Reform Association was founded in America in 1845 by George Henry Evans, publisher of the *Working Mans Advocate*. It advocated a ten-hour day, land-nationalization, suppression of profiteering and abolition of slavery.

bath breaking Puritans. I will give you a specimen of it from a recent report of the Church Pastoral Aid Society. President, Lord Ashley. Vice presidents, a set of landed Aristocrats, Capitalists and State priests. Concerning this Pastoral-aid Society, it is a remarkable fact, that a Church possessing a yearly revenue of about ten millions sterling, for the purpose of paying men to teach its doctrines to the English people, should yet find it necessary to raise funds by subscription. One reverend gent, who recently received £70 for a lay assistant, reports that his is the incumbent of a district, supposed to contain about 20,000 souls, and that, *"the moral condition of it is deplorable. Socialism, Infidelity, Rationalism, and indifference prevail to a fearful extent"*. He gives some anecdotes of this, and concludes thus:

> *a third individual, when warned to flee from the wrath to come, said—'Let us hope there is no such place as hellfire, and no such awful work as gnashing of teeth for us poor creatures. We have too much misery to endure here, for God to think of punishing us hereafter'. These instances are types of the general depravity.*

Can the force of humbug further go? Not content with the social degradation of the wage-slaves, this ruthless pharisee must needs threaten them with 'the wrath to come'. Truly, I think the People have suffered enough from 'the wrath' at present—that is, from being mercilessly used up by the State patrons of such pious humbugs as the above—and there is little need of 'the wrath to come'. But what a state of things!

On the one hand, the producers ground down under a regularly organized system of plunder; on the other, a set of State priests kept for the purpose of inducing them to submit quietly to all this horrible suffering, by the promise of a good life hereafter in heaven or the threat of torments in hell-fire! Another of these Evangelical gentry is laughably naïve in his report. He complains of the spread of Mormonism in his district, but accounts for it *"by the preference men have for the marvellous, and desire of possessing heaven here on earth, toiling in our rumbling manufactories, and being subject to authority and rule"*.[1] The Mormons are subject to a very strict, semi-military discipline, but *every* member of a Mor-

---

1. By 1850, the Mormon Church had more members in England (about 50,000) than in the USA (27,000). English Mormonism went into decline during the 1850s because most of the converts emigrated

mon Association is certain of being comfortably fed, housed, and clothed. Certainly a 'heaven here on earth', when compared with the condition of the English Proletarians. I believe Joe Smith's tenets partake somewhat of the marvellous, but this Mormon Apostle must have been a stunning fellow, if he produced anything more astonishing than the Creed of St. Athanasius.[1] The Moral—my Proletarian brothers—to be deduced from this disquisition on secular and priestly Humbug, is simply this. Do not expect help from any other class than your own. Do not reckon upon being emancipated through other efforts than your own. Do not waste time in trying to make converts to Chartism among the so-called 'respectable' portion of society—that is, in any other class than *your own. Do not throw your pearls before swine.*

---

to the USA, and because the church was scandalised by revelations concerning Joseph Smith's polygamous practices.

1. Athanasius of Alexandria (c.296–373), is traditionally held to have formulated the Doctrine of the Holy Trinity in opposition to the Arians, whom he denounced as heretics at Emperor Constantine's Council of Nicea in 325.

Friend of the People

21 & 26 December 1850

Signs of the Times. Red-Stockings *versus* Lawn-Sleeves

Friend of the People, 21 & 26 December 1850

Part one

Old Mother Church is all in a twitter at the bare idea of certain naughty Popish attempts to poach on her sacred manor.[1] A fearful shriek of clerical woe has been raised from one end of England to the other, while faithful Protestants have duly responded to the call of the 'pulpit drum ecclesiastic' by frantic 'No Popery' battle shouts, and the sacrifice of innumerable Guys. Any act of the imbecile old man, who at present so unworthily occupies the chair of Gregory the Great—or any amount of silly fanatical clamour that could be raised in this silly fanatical country of ours, would be unworthy of your notice, my Proletarian Brothers—were it not that these things have elicited an expression of opinion from two 'illustrious personages', two

---

1. In September 1850 Pope Pius IX decided to re-establish a full Catholic hierarchy in England and Wales for the first time since the reign of Mary Tudor (1555–1558) and appointed Cardinal Nicholas Wiseman (1802–1865) as Archbishop of Westminster. Following Wiseman's statement, "*Catholic England has been restored to its orbit in the ecclesiastical firmament, from which its light had long vanished*", there were widespread 'No-Popery' protests by Anglicans, and Prime Minister Lord John Russell railed against 'papal aggression'. At the time, the Church of England was still reeling from the defections to Catholicism of the eminent Anglican theologian, John Henry Newman, and his followers.

of the highest authorities *"as by law established in Church and State"*; namely, from the Bishop of London [Charles Blomfield], and [Prime Minister] Lord John Russell. Constitutional authorities both—repositories of the accumulated 'wisdom of our ancestors'—surely if a solution of the great question of the age is to be looked for at all, we might look for it at such hands. And if the rulers of society have not the remotest glimpse of the idea agitating the minds of those they aspire to govern—not the faintest notion of the social problem of the age they pretend to direct and represent—they should have the grace to remain silent. But the Bishop rambles in a distracted manner through a 'charge' about the size of an octavo volume, the Whig Prime Minister fills a long letter with the silliest twaddle about *"a nation which has so nobly vindicated its right to freedom of opinion, civil, political, and religious"*; yet neither of these gentlemen really say *anything*, though they speak at great length. Both the Bishop and the Minister are extremely alarmed, but it is satisfactory to learn that the 'alarm' of the latter, is *"not equal to his indignation"*; and that he relies on *"a nation which looks with scorn at the laborious endeavours which are now making to confine the intellect and enslave the soul"*.

Well crowed, little Bantam! A shrill blast that on the trumpet of constitutional Whiggery, a good specimen of public-dinner liberal claptrap! How dare any one—even a Whig official—prate about *Freedom*, when the laws relating to sedition and high treason are so loosely framed (*purposely*, I opine) that any protest against the present shameful system of class legislation, of misgovernment and no-government, can be construed as treason, and punished by transportation and imprisonment? Whilst, on the one hand, the felon's doom—on the other, the persecution and hatred of the 'respectable classes', await all those who affirm that the Proletarian is also a human being; that wages-slavery ought to be abolished: that the PEOPLE ought to have an equal share with the privileged, legalised horde of bandits, who have hitherto monopolized *all* the advantages of civilization—whilst this is the case, it is an insolent mockery to talk of *Freedom*. The felon's doom, did I say? Murderers are never starved to death—like Sharp and Williams; thieves are not insulted—like Ernest Jones.[1] It disgusts one to hear the sacred name of Freedom thus

---

1. Chartist leaders Alexander Sharpe, Joseph Williams and Ernst Jones were at this time serving prison sentences for making 'seditious'

blasphemed; the highest and noblest law of Humanity profaned by a 'red-tape talking machine', who babbles he knows not what.[1] Evidently, there is no solution of any problem whatsoever to be expected from such a source. Poor governor of *practical* England in the *enlightened* nineteenth century! Do Whig chimeras of 'freedom, civil, religious, and political'—feed the hungry, clothe the naked, or empty the jails and workhouses which have been filled by leaving ignorance and famine to make their home in the dwellings of the poor? Will all this preaching about constitutional fictions—now fast becoming an intolerable nuisance—will it reclaim the 15 million acres of land at present lying waste and useless, but which would, if properly cultivated *with the spade* furnish the means of comfortable subsistence for 60 millions of 'surplus population?' Yet no! prate, prate, prate, goes his lordship—like all their lordships, past, present, or to come. A chattering, mischievous magpie, with a constitutional chorus of 658 geese. Turn we now to the Bishop. Let us see in what way a spiritual guide of men in these distracted times proposes to aid our temporal head in resisting the papistical efforts *"which are now making to confine the intellect and enslave the soul"*. How does old Mother Church come up to the rescue? Why, as I think, in a very inefficient, hobbling limping, sort of way. The aim of Popery being the confining and enslaving of the intellect and soul, I presume the aim of the Anglican Church and of all true Protestants is the opposite of this; namely, the enlargement and liberation of the intellect and soul. How then, does the Bishop propose to further this Protestant aim? Simply, by stifling all free thought, all free inquiry, by preventing the development of the intellectual and moral nature of man beyond the limits of a few narrow episcopalian symbols and dogmas; by 'confining the intellect and soul' strictly within the inviolable precincts of the Thirty-nine Articles! In this 'Charge' (of the church militant), I find the following astonishing sentence—the Bishop, after premising that the Latin Church addresses herself to the senses of men by 'mummeries', and to their understandings by *"subtle dialecticians and persuasive orators"*—hopes that *"none of you will give the least countenance to*

---

speeches at Clerkenwell Green and Bishop Bonner's Fields.
1. Thomas Carlyle, in *Latter-Day Pamphlets*, referred to British politics as *"Little other than a red tape Talking-machine, and unhappy Bag of Parliamentary Eloquence"*.

their proceedings nor run the risk of impairing the strength of your own convictions, and of weakening your attachment to the Church of which you are members, by attending any of their services, or listening to their lectures". For the Thirty-nine Articles substitute the decisions of the Council of Trent, for the Anglican Bishop substitute the Romish Cardinal—and then show me in what the two churches—the Papist and the so-called Protestant—differ.[1] They unite in repudiating the principle of free enquiry; they both impose an *outward* restraint upon the mind; they both assume that points of faith ought to be decided by some other authority than that of individual men, *each for himself.*

Part two

My Proletarian Brothers, this case of Red-stockings *versus* Lawn-sleeves, wherein the Lawn-sleeves have *openly* assumed a most illogical and absurd position, is among the most important and cheering signs of the times.[2] Because it shows that the world of Ideas is taking the same direction as the world of Facts. The *inward* world is obeying the same law as the *outward* world. The modern middle-class system of production and distribution is constantly tending towards the destruction of the small capitalist, the master tradesman, the retail shopkeeper, the small manufacturer, etc., tending towards the division of society into the two great classes of rich and poor, capitalist and wages slaves, privileged and unprivileged, financial, aristocrat, and proletarian. When this division is accomplished, a servile war will be the inevitable result. The two hostile armies must fight out the last of the innumerable class-battles, and the victory will be to the strongest class—to the revolutionary proletariat. They are the Men of the Future, and the task entrusted to them as the re-organisation of society, the creation of a new heavens and a new earth, when the old shall have been 'rolled up like a scroll', and utterly abolished. I have said the inward world is obeying the same law. The world of thought is rapidly breaking up into two camps; the one containing the partisans of despotic authority; the other, the champions

---

1. Between 1545 and 1563, the Council of Trent issued condemnations of Protestant heresies and attempted to clearly define Church teachings and practices.
2. Red stockings are worn by Catholic cardinals; lawn-sleeves by Anglican bishops.

of unlimited free thought; of *unlimited, unchecked, intellectual, and moral development*. Now, one effect of this spiritual movement will be, that the partisans of intellectual despotism, (*who are also invariably the upholders of secular despotism*) will no longer get leave to masquerade among the defenders of liberty. Protestantism must now accept the reformation of the nineteenth century, or enter the Camp of the Past. The present weak and contemptible aspect of Protestantism is the result of the miserable compromise between truth and falsehood—the halting between two opinions—which has been going on ever since the Reformation of the sixteenth century. The more logical and sincere class of minds, in England as well as in Germany, has come to similar conclusions. On all sides, thinking men are either re-entering the pale of Rome, or throwing off the whole superstructure of scholastic theology as a dead weight, which impedes the healthy action of their minds, as something which is worse than useless. Here then, we see the dawn of the new reformation; we have the tendencies of the present age developed in the form of two frightful bugbears; on the one hand, appearing as the Catholicism; on the other, as the *"Rationalism with infidelity and Pantheism in it train"*,—which are now exciting a flutter of holy fervour among the Lawn-sleeves, and causing every hair on venerable episcopal wigs to become instinct with pious indignation, and stand on end—*"like quills upon the fretful porcupine"*.[1]

But the days of orthodox Protestantism are now numbered. The human mind has not been standing still for the last 300 years. Men are beginning to perceive that this system satisfies neither the heart nor the head; neither the imagination nor the intellect. For it swept away all the poetry of the Christian Mythos, and gave a death blow to the art of the Middle Ages. It left us nothing but a set of abstract creeds and dogmas, professedly based upon another set of questionable sagas and hearsays. Nothing save a museum of old dried up scholastic formulas; which, however they might express the convictions, or reflect back the consciousness of man in the sixteenth century, have been outgrown

---

1. Shakespeare, *Hamlet*, Act I, Scene 5:
   Ghost: *Make thy two eyes, like stars, start from their spheres,*
   Thy knotted and combined locks to part,
   And each particular hair to stand on end,
   Like quills upon the fretful porcupine.

by him in the nineteenth, and are now so many impediments to his spiritual development. Yet, as every historical appearance, every manifestation of a thought, is (in its place) both useful and inevitable—or, in other words, *as every fact has a meaning*, you will naturally ask, what is the meaning of Protestantism? It is a state of transition. It is the necessary stepping-stone for the human mind in its progress from deism to pantheism—that is, from the belief in the holiness of *some* things, in the divinity of *one* being or of *one* man, to a belief in the divinity of *All* beings, of *All* men— in the holiness of *All* things. The reformation of the sixteenth century having remained stationary between spiritual despotism and spiritual freedom, found its befitting complement, *its secular mode of expression*, in the form of government called constitutional. The inward or spiritual compromise between these principles of the past and the future, resulted in the outward or temporal compromise between the same. A stunted, crippled idea *could* produce nothing better than a miserable ghastly abortion of balance of powers, king, lords, and commons, constitutional fictions, whig prime ministers—and the like. All history bears witness to the truth of an old saying—'as a man is, so are his gods';[1] or conversely, that the actions of man—the laws, forms of government, art, literature, manners, and customs, in a word, *the phases of civilisation*, prevalent amongst any people, are directly derived from its theology. If we know the fundamental principle of any given theology, we can at once predict the amount of secular freedom, *or the degree of political and social development*—which is compatible with a belief in that theology. Thus, we find feudal despotism the prevailing form of government in Catholic countries. It is the secular expression for that principle of absolute spiritual authority of which Catholicism is the only logical, consequent, and satisfactory development. In the regions of spiritual compromise, of doubt and fluctuation, of unrest, of weariness and vexation of the soul—in the regions of Protestantism, (protesting against error, yet stopping short of truth) we find in secular things, a like system of unsatisfactory compromise, of incessant fluctuation. There is no fundamental principle, upon which a reasonable creature could find a firm footing—concerning which he could say, "I see what this is, I accept or reject it with all its consequences".

---

1. *"As a man is, so is his God; therefore God was so often an object of mockery."* Goethe, *Penguin Poets* series, 1964, p. 262.

I find, not only in the Anglican Church, but as the fatal absurdity which pervades the whole Protestant system—I find that an infallible Book is assumed as the basis of religious faith, yet without having any *professedly* infallible interpreter. *Covertly* every sect assumes its own articles, confession, or creed, to be the infallible interpreter; and if any one dare to read the *"Bible, which is the religion of Protestants"* otherwise than through a pair of sectarian spectacles, he is immediately denounced as 'an infidel scoffer', and held up to public execration. Is not this incredible logic? I infinitely prefer the logic of the Romish Cardinal, who says— *"Do not read this infallible book, for the Church is the only authorised interpreter"*. If a religion *based upon historic evidences*—upon matters of critical research and antiquarian learning, things—that is—beyond the reach of any but the most highly educated portion of society—if an *Historical* religion is to be *religion for the masses, a universal religion*, then it must have a perpetually inspired (or infallible) witness for its truth. That witness is the Church! Is not a man who puts a book into the hands of Tom, Dick, and Harry, telling them to read it diligently—and then denounces them for having different opinions about it from those he himself entertains, is he not a donkey of the first magnitude? Why does Lawn-sleeves give us the book at all? *His* opinions are the only 'evangelical and saving' ones, when all is done. In Constitutional Governments, (the secular side of the intellectual fiction called Protestantism,) there is a similar fatal absurdity. Constitutional liberty for *some* but not for *all*. The power, wealth, and cultivation of civilized society are concentrated within the narrow limits of certain classes. The Suffrage, for example, is capriciously distributed according to notions of whig expediency, finality, Reform Bills, and the like. But the new religion, that of unlimited spiritual freedom—whose dawn is now visible, whose banner bears the sacred inscription, Equality, Liberty, Fraternity—will also find a befitting secular mode of expression. It will bring in its train corresponding institutions and social forms. It will assume the outward form of a republic such as the world has never yet seen. 'A republic without helots';[1] without *poor*; with-

---

1. The phrase, 'Republic Without Helots', comes from August Blanqui's speech to the French court in 1849, which was translated and published in Harney's *Friend of the People*, 26 July, 1851: "... *it is said, labour currency, and credit are affairs of political economy and not of feeling. I know not, but faith and enthusiasm are lovers to move the world from its*

out *classes*; without hereditary hewers of wood and drawers of water; without *slaves*, whether chattel or wages slaves. *"For if I treat all men as divine, how can there be for me such a thing as a slave?"* A society, such indeed as the world has never yet seen—not only of free men, but of free *women*; a society of equally holy, equally blessed gods.[1]

---

foundations. Let us begin there, the rest will follow. Alexander, in the desert of Gedrosia, scattered on the sand some water that was brought to him in a helmet, exclaiming, "Every one, or no one!" The self-denial of the General electrified the dispirited Macedonian army it and saved it by inspiring courage and hope. When the people are starving, no one ought to eat. This is my utopia, my dream in the February Days. It raised up against me the heat of implacable enemies. I wished to touch the consciences of men; they only thought of letting loose conflicting class interests. Yet the question was not that of a Republic of Spartans, but of a Republic without Helots. Perhaps my utopia will appear the most absurd and the most impossible of all. Then may God have mercy on France!"

1. This phrase—"A society, such indeed as the world has never seen—not only of free men, but of free women; a society of equally, holy, equally blessed gods"— borrows from Heinrich Heine's essay 'The New Pantheism' (1835):

> *The political revolution which is based on the principles of French materialism will find no enemies in the pantheists, but rather allies who derive their convictions from a deeper source, from a religious synthesis... [The] divinity of man manifests itself also in his body. Human misery destroys or abases the body, which is the image of God... We do not wish to be sans-culottes, or frugal citizens, or economical presidents. We establish a democracy of equally glorious, equally holy and equally happy gods. You ask for simple dress, austere manners and unseasoned joys. We, on the other hand, demand nectar and ambrosia, purple raiments, costly perfumes, luxury and splendour, dances of laughing nymphs, music and comedy. Oh, do not be angry, virtuous republicans! To your censorious reproaches, we say with the fool in Shakespeare, "Dost thou think because thou art virtuous, there shall be no more cakes and ale?"... We have, in fact outgrown deism. We are free and do not need a tyrant with thunder. We have come of age and do not need paternal supervision. We are not the bungled handiwork of a great mechanic. Deism is a religion for slaves, children, Genevans and watchmakers.*

Heinrich Heine, *Self Portrait* (essays) p. 560.

*Membership Card for the National
Charter Association*

Red Republican

November 1850

THE RED REPUBLICAN.

EQUALITY, LIBERTY, FRATERNITY.

EDITED BY G. JULIAN HARNEY.

No. 21.—Vol. I.]   SATURDAY, NOVEMBER 9, 1850.   [PRICE ONE PENNY.

German Communism.

MANIFESTO OF THE GERMAN COMMUNIST PARTY.

(Published in February, 1848.)

THE following Manifesto, which has since been adopted by all fractions of German Communists, was drawn up in the German language, in January 1848, by Citizens *Charles Marx* and *Frederic Engels*. It was immediately printed in London, in the German language, and published a few days before the outbreak of the Revolution of February. The turmoil consequent upon that great event made it impossible to carry out, at that time, the intention of translating it into all the languages of civilized Europe. There exist two different French versions of it in manuscript, but under the present oppressive laws of France, the publication of either of them has been found impracticable. The English reader will be enabled, by the following excellent translation of this important document, to judge of the plans and principles of the most advanced party of the German Revolutionists.

It must not be forgotten, that the whole of this Manifesto was written and printed before the Revolution of February.

A frightful hobgoblin stalks throughout Europe. We are haunted by a ghost, the ghost of Communism. All the Powers of the Past have joined in a holy crusade to lay this ghost to rest,—the Pope and the Czar, Metternich and Guizot, French Radicals and German police agents. Where is the opposition which has not been accused of Communism by its enemies in Power? And where the opposition that has not hurled this blighting accusation at the hands of the more advanced oppositionists, as well as at those of its official enemies?

Two things appear on considering these facts.
1. The ruling Powers of Europe acknowledge Communism to be also a Power. 2. It is time for the Communists to lay before the world an account of their aims and tendencies, and to oppose these idle fables about the bugbear of Communism, by a manifesto of the Communist Party.

CHAPTER I.

BOURGEOIS AND PROLETARIANS.

HITHERTO the history of Society has been the history of the battles between the classes composing it. Freemen and Slaves, Patricians and Plebeians, Nobles and Serfs, Members of Guilds and journeymen,—in a word, the oppressors and the oppressed, have always stood in direct opposition to each other. The battle between them has sometimes been open, sometimes concealed, but always continuous. A never-ceasing battle, which has invariably ended, either in a revolutionary alteration of the social system, or in the common destruction of the battle classes.

In the earlier historical epochs we find almost everywhere a minute division of Society into classes or ranks, a variety of grades in social position. In ancient Rome we find Patricians, Knights, Plebeians, Slaves; in medieval Europe, Feudal Lords, Vassals, Burghers, Journeymen, Serfs; and in each of these classes there were again grades and distinctions. Modern Bourgeois Society, proceeded from the ruins of the feudal system, but the Bourgeois regime has not abolished the antagonism of classes.

New classes, new conditions of oppression, new forms and modes of carrying on the struggle, have been substituted for the old ideas. The characteristic of our Epoch, the Era of the Middle-class, or Bourgeoisie, is that the struggle between the various Social Classes, has been reduced to its simplest form. Society incessantly tends to be divided into two great camps, into two great hostile armies, the Bourgeoisie and the Proletariat.

The Burgesses of the early Communes sprang from the Serfs of the Middle Ages, and from this Municipal class were developed the primitive elements of the modern Bourgeoisie. The discovery of the New World, the circumnavigation of Africa, gave the Middle-class—then coming into being—new fields of action. The colonisation of America, the opening up of the East Indian and Chinese Markets, the Colonial Trade, the increase of commodities generally and of the means of exchange, gave an impetus, hitherto unknown, to Commerce, Shipping, and Manufactures; and aided the rapid evolution of the revolutionary element in the old decaying, feudal form of Society. The old feudal way of managing the industrial interest by means of guilds and monopolies was not found sufficient for the increased demand caused by the opening up of these new markets. It was replaced by the manufacturing system. Guilds vanished before the industrial Middle-class, and the division of labour between the different corporations was succeeded by the division of labour between the workmen of one and the same great workshop.

But the demand always increased, new markets came into play. The manufacturing system, in its turn, was found to be inadequate. At this point industrial Production was revolutionised by machinery and steam. The modern industrial system was developed in all its gigantic proportions; instead of the industrial Middle-class we find industrial millionaires, chiefs of whole industrial armies, the modern Bourgeois, or Middle-class Capitalists. The discovery of America was the first step towards the formation of a colonial market, increasing the whole world, wherever an immense development was given to Commerce, and to our means of communication by sea and land. This again reacted upon the industrial system, and the development of the Bourgeoisie, the increase of their Capital, the superseding of all classes handed down by modern times from the Middle Ages, kept pace with the development of Production, Trade, and Steam communication.

We find, therefore, that the modern Bourgeoisie are themselves the result of a long process of development, of a series of revolutions in the modes of Production and Exchanges. Each of the degrees of industrial evolution, passed through by the modern Middle-class, was accompanied by a corresponding

Introduction by George Julian Harney

George Julian Harney
Red Republican, **9 November 1850**.

The following Manifesto, which has since been adopted by all fractions of German Communists, was drawn up in the German language, in January 1848, by Citizens Charles Marx and Frederic Engels. It was immediately printed in London, in the German language, and published a few days before the outbreak of the Revolution of February. The turmoil consequent upon that great event made it impossible to carry out, at that time, the intention of translating it into all the languages of civilized Europe. There exist two different French versions of it in manuscript, but under the present oppressive laws of France, the publication of either of them has been found impracticable. The English reader will be enabled, by the following excellent translation of this important document, to judge of the plans and principles of the most advanced party of the German Revolutionists. It must not be forgotten, that the whole of this Manifesto was written and printed before the Revolution of February.[1]

---

1. Not until 1872 was it publicly revealed by Marx and Engels in their preface to the German edition of the Manifesto that it *"was published in the English for the first time in 1850 in* The Red Republican, *translated by Miss Helen Macfarlane"*.

Manifesto of the German Communist Party

Marx and Engels, translated by Helen Macfarlane
Red Republican, 9, 16, 23 & 30 November 1850

A frightful hobgoblin stalks throughout Europe. We are haunted by a ghost, the ghost of Communism. All the Powers of the Past have joined in a holy crusade to lay this ghost to rest—the Pope and the Czar, Metternich and Guizot, French Radicals and German police agents.

Where is the opposition which has not been accused of Communism by its enemies in Power? And where the opposition that has not hurled this blighting accusation at the heads of the more advanced oppositionists, as well as at those of its official enemies?

Two things appear on considering these facts.

1) The ruling Powers of Europe acknowledge Communism to be also a Power.
2) It is time for the Communists to lay before the world an account of their aims and tendencies and to oppose these silly fables about *"the bugbear of Communism"* by a manifesto of the Communist Party.

[To this end, Communists of various nationalities have assembled in London and sketched the following manifesto, to be published in the English, French, German, Italian, Flemish and Danish languages.][1]

---

1. This sentence from the original German edition (Moore translation, 1872) is omitted from the Macfarlane translation.

Chapter one: bourgeois and proletarians

Hithertofore the history of Society has been the history of the battle between the classes composing it. Freemen and Slaves, Patricians and Plebeians, Nobles and Serfs, Members of Guilds and Journeymen—in a word, the oppressors and the oppressed, have always stood in direct opposition to each other. The battle between them has sometimes been open, sometimes concealed, but always continuous. A never-ceasing battle, which has invariably ended, either in a revolutionary alteration of the social system, or in the common destruction of the hostile classes.

In the earlier historical epochs we find almost everywhere a minute division of Society into classes or ranks, a variety of grades in social position. In ancient Rome we find Patricians, Knights, Plebeians, Slaves, in Mediaeval Europe, Feudal Lords, Vassals, Burghers, Journeymen, Serfs; and in each of these classes there were again grades and distinctions. Modern Bourgeois Society, proceeded from the ruins if the feudal system, but the Bourgeois regime has not abolished the antagonism of classes.

New classes, new conditions of oppression, new forms and modes of carrying on the struggle, have been substituted for the old ones. The characteristic of our Epoch, the Era of the Middle-class, or Bourgeoisie, is that struggle between the various Social Classes has been reduced to its simplest form. Society incessantly tends to be divided into two great camps, into two great hostile armies, the Bourgeoisie and the Proletariat.

The burgesses of the early Communes sprang from the Serfs of the Middle Ages. From the Municipal class were developed the primitive elements of the modern Bourgeoisie. The discovery of the New World, the circumnavigation of Africa, gave the Middle class—then coming into being—new fields of action. The colonization of America, the opening up of the East Indian and Chinese markets, the Colonial Trade. The increase of commodities generally and of the means of exchange, gave an impetus, hitherto unknown, to Commerce, Shipping and the revolutionary element in the old decaying feudal form of society. The old feudal way of managing the industrial interest by means of guilds and monopolies was not found sufficient for the increased demand caused by the opening up of these new markets. It was replaced by the manufacturing system. Guilds vanished before the industrial Middle-class, and the division of labour between the different corporations was succeeded by the division of labour between the workmen of one and the same great workshop.

But the demand always increased, new markets came into play. The manufacturing system, in its turn, was found to be inadequate. At this point industrial Production was revolutionised by machinery and steam. The modern industrial system was developed in all its gigantic proportions; instead of the industrial Middle-class we find industrial millionaires, chiefs of whole industrial armies, the modern Bourgeois, or Middle-class Capitalists. The discovery of America was the first step towards the formation of a colossal market, embracing the whole world; whereby an immense development of the Bourgeoisie, the increase of their Capital, the superseding of all classes handed down to modern times from the Middle Ages, kept pace with the development of Production, Trade, and Steam communication.

We find, therefore, that the modern Bourgeoisie are themselves the result of a long process of development, of a series of revolutions in the modes of Production and Exchange. Each of the degrees of industrial revolution, passed through by the modern Middle-class, was accompanied by a corresponding degree of political development. This class was oppressed under the feudal regime, it then assumed the form of armed and self-regulating associations in the medieval Municipalities; in one country we find it existing as a commercial republic, or free town; in another, as the third taxable Estate of the Monarchy; then during the prevalence of the manufacturing system (before the introduction of steam power) the Middle-class was a counterpoise to the Nobility in absolute Monarchies, and the groundwork of the powerful monarchical States generally. Finally, since the establishment of the modern industrial system, with its world-wide market, this class has gained the exclusive possession of political power in modern representative States. Modern Governments are merely Committees for managing the common affairs of the whole Bourgeoisie.

This Bourgeoisie has occupied an extremely revolutionary position in History. As soon as the Bourgeois got the upper hand, they destroyed all feudal, patriarchal, idyllic relationships between men. They relentlessly tore asunder the many-sided links of that feudal chain which bound men to their 'natural superiors', and they left no bond of union between man and man, save that of bare self-interest, of cash payments. They changed personal dignity into market value, and substituted the single unprincipled freedom of trade for the numerous, hardly earned, chartered liberties of the Middle Ages. Chivalrous enthusiasm, the emotions of piety, vanished before the icy breath of their selfish calculations. In a word, the Bourgeoisie substituted shameless, direct, open spoliation, for the previous system of spoliation concealed under religious and political illusions. They stripped off that halo of sanctity which had surrounded the various modes of human activity, and had made them venerable, and venerated. They changed the physician, the jurisprudent, the priest, the poet, the philosopher, into their hired servants. They tore the touching veil of sentiment from domestic ties, and reduced family-relations to a mere question of hard cash. The Middle-classes have shown how the brutal physical force of the Middle Ages, so much admired by Reactionists, found its befitting complement in the laziest ruffianism. They have also shown what human activity is capable of accomplishing. They have done quite other kinds of marvellous work than Egyptian pyramids, Roman aqueducts, or Gothic Cathedrals; and their expeditions have far surpassed all former Crusades, and Migrations of nations.

The Bourgeoisie can exist only under the condition of continuously revolutionising machinery, or the instruments of Production. That is, perpetually changing the system of production, which again amounts to changing the whole system of social arrangements. Persistence in the old modes of Production was, on the contrary, the first condition of existence for all the preceding industrial Classes. A continual change in the modes of Production, a never ceasing state of agitation and social insecurity, distinguish the Bourgeois-Epoch from all preceding ones. The ancient ties between men, their opinions and beliefs—hoar with antiquity—are fast disappearing, and the new ones become worn out ere they can become firmly rooted. Every thing fixed and stable vanishes, everything holy and venerable is desecrated, and men are forced to look at their mutual relations, at the problem of Life, in the soberest, the most matter of fact way.

The need of an ever-increasing market for their produce drives the Bourgeoisie over the whole globe—they are forced to make settlements, to form connections, to set up means of communication everywhere. Through their command of a universal market, they have given a cosmopolitan tendency to the production and consumption of all countries. To the great regret of the Reactionists, the Bourgeoisie have deprived the modern Industrial System of its national foundation. The old national manufactures have been, or are being, destroyed. They are superseded by new modes of industry, whose introduction is becoming a vital question for all civilized nations, whose raw materials are not indigenous, but are brought from the remotest countries, and whose products are not merely consumed in the home market, but throughout the whole world. Instead of the old national wants, supplied by indigenous products, we everywhere find new wants, which can be supplied only by the productions of the remotest lands and climes. Instead of the old local and national feeling of self-sufficingness and isolation, we find a universal intercourse, an inter-dependence, amongst nations. The same fact obtains in the intellectual world. The intellectual productions of individual nations tend to become common property. National one-sidedness and mental limitation are fast becoming impossible, and a universal literature is being formed from the numerous national and local literatures. Through the incessant improvements in machinery and the means of locomotion, the Bourgeoisie draw the most barbarous savages into the magic circle of civilization. Cheap goods are their artillery for battering down Chinese walls, and their means of overcoming the obstinate hatred entertained towards strangers by semi-civilized nations. The Bourgeoisie, by their competition, compel, under penalty of inevitable ruin, the universal adoption of their system of production; they force all nations to accept what is called civilization—to become Bourgeois—and thus the middle class fashions the world anew after its own image.

The Bourgeoisie has subjected the country to the ascendancy of the town; it has created enormous cities, and, by causing an immense increase of population in the manufacturing, as compared with the agricultural districts, has saved a great part of every people from the idiotism of country life. Not only have the Bourgeoisie made the country subordinate to the town, they have made barbarous and half-civilized tribes dependent on civilized nations, the agricultural on the manufacturing nations, the East on the West. The division of property, of the means of production, and of population, vanish under the Bourgeois regime. It agglomerates population, it centralises the means of production, and concentrates property in the hands of a few individuals. Political centralization is the necessary consequence of this. Independent provinces, with different interests, each of them surrounded by a separate line of customs and under separate local governments, are brought together as one nation, under the same government, laws, line of customs, tariff, the same national class-interest. The Bourgeois regime has only prevailed for about a century, but during that time it has called into being more gigantic powers of production than all preceding generations put together. The subjection of the elements of nature, the development of machinery, the application of chemistry to agriculture and manufactures, railways, electric telegraphs, steam ships, the clearing and cultivation of whole continents, canalizing of thousands of rivers; large populations, whole industrial armies, springing up, as if by magic! What preceding generation ever dreamed of these productive powers slumbering within society?

We have seen that these means of production and traffic which served as the foundation of middle-class development, originated in feudal times. At a certain point in the evolution of these means, the arrangements under which feudal society produced and exchanged the feudal organisation of agriculture and industrial production—in a word, the feudal conditions of property—no longer corresponded to the increased productive power. These conditions now became a hindrance to it—they were turned into fetters which had to be broken, and they were broken. They were superseded by unlimited competition, with a suitable social and political constitution, with the economical and political supremacy of the middle class.

At the present moment a similar movement is going on before our eyes. Modern middle-class society, which has revolutionised the conditions of property, and called forth such colossal means of production and traffic, resembles the wizard who evoked the powers of darkness, but could neither master them, nor yet get rid of them when they had come at his bidding. The history of manufactures and commerce has been for many years the history of the revolts of modern productive power against the modern industrial system—against the modern conditions of property—which are vital conditions, not only of the supremacy of the middle-class, but of its very existence. It suffices to mention the commercial crises which, in each of their periodical occurrences, more and more endanger the existence of middle-class society. In such a crisis, not only is a quantity of industrial products destroyed, but a large portion of the productive power itself.

A social epidemic breaks out, the epidemic of over-production, which would have appeared a contradiction in terms to all previous generations. Society finds itself suddenly thrown back into momentary barbarism; a famine, a devastating war, seems to have deprived it of the means of subsistence; manufactures and commerce appear annihilated—and why? Because society possesses too much civilisation, too many of the necessaries of life, too much industry, too much commerce.

The productive power possessed by society no longer serves as the instrument of middle-class civilization, of the middle-class conditions of property; on the contrary, this power has become too mighty for this system, it is forcibly confined by these conditions; and whenever it surpasses these artificial limitations, it deranges the system of Bourgeois society, it endangers the existence of Bourgeois property. The social system of the middle-class has become too small to contain the riches it has called into being. How does the middle-class try to withstand these commercial crises? On the one hand, by destroying masses of productive power; on the other, by opening up new markets, and using up the old ones more thoroughly. That is, they prepare the way for still more universal and dangerous crises, and reduce the means of withstanding them. The weapons with which the middle-class overcame feudalism are now turned against the middle-class itself. And the Bourgeoisie have not only prepared the weapons for their own destruction, they have also called into existence the men that are destined to wield these weapons, namely, the modern working men, the Proletarians.

The development of the Proletariat has kept pace with the development of the middle-class—that is, with the development of capital; for the modern working men can live only as long as they find work, and they find it only as long as their labour increases capital. These workers, who must sell themselves by piecemeal to the highest bidder, are a commodity like other articles of commerce, and, therefore, are equally subject to all the variations of the market, and the effects of competition. Through the division of labour and the extension of machinery, work has lost its individual character, and therefore its interest for the operative. He has become merely an accessory to, or a part of the machine, and all that is required of him is a fatiguing, monotonous, and merely mechanical operation. The expense the wages-slave causes the capitalist is, therefore, equal to the cost of his keep and of the propagation of his race. The price of labour, like that of any other commodity, is equal to the cost of its production. Therefore wages decrease in proportion as the work to be performed becomes mechanical, monotonous, fatiguing, and repulsive. Further, in proportion as the application of machinery and the division of labour increase, the amount of work increases also, whether it be through an increase in the hours of work, or in the quantity of it demanded in a given time, or through an increased rate of velocity of the machinery employed.

The modern industrial system has changed the little shop of the primitive patriarchal master into the large factory of the Bourgeois-capitalist. Masses of operatives are brought together in one establishment, and organized like a regiment of soldiers; they are placed under the superintendence of a complete hierarchy of officers and sub-officers. They are not only the slaves of the whole middle-class (as a body), of the Bourgeois political regime—they are the daily and hourly slaves of the machinery, of the foreman, of each individual manufacturing Bourgeois. This despotism is the more hateful, contemptible, and aggravating, because gain is openly proclaimed to be its only object and aim. In proportion as labour requires less physical force and less dexterity—that is, in proportion to the development of the modern industrial system—is the substitution of the labour of women and children for that of men. The distinctions of sex and age have no social meaning for the Proletarian class. Proletarians are merely so many instruments which cost more or less, according to their sex and age. When the using-up of the operative has been so far accomplished by the mill-owner that the former has got his wages, the rest of the Bourgeoisie, householders, shopkeepers, pawnbrokers, etc., fall upon him like so many harpies.

The petty Bourgeoisie, the inferior ranks of the middle-class, the small manufacturers, merchants, tradesmen, and farmers, tend to become Proletarians, partly because their small capital succumbs to the competition of the millionaire, and partly because, the modes of production perpetually changing, their peculiar skill loses its value. Thus the Proletariat is recruited from various sections of the population.

This Proletarian class passes through many phases of development, but its struggle with the middle-class dates from its birth. At first the struggle is carried on by individual workmen, then by those belonging to a single establishment, then by those of an entire trade in the same locality, against the individuals of the middle-class who directly use them up. They attack not only the middle-class system of production, but even the instruments of production; they destroy machinery and the foreign commodities which compete with their products; they burn down factories, and try to re-attain the position occupied by the producers of the middle ages. At this moment of development, the Proletariat forms a disorganized mass, scattered throughout the country, and divided by competition. A more compact union is not the effect of their own development, but is the consequence of a middle-class union; for the Bourgeoisie requires, and for the moment are still enabled, to set the whole Proletariat in motion, for the furtherance of their own political ends; developed in this degree, therefore, the Proletarians do not fight their own enemies, but the enemies of their enemies, the remains of absolute monarchy, the land-owners, the non-manufacturing part of the Bourgeoisie and the petty shopocracy.

The whole historical movement is thus, as yet, concentrated in the hands of the Bourgeoisie, every victory is won for them. But the increase of the Proletariat keeps pace with the evolution of production; the working-class is brought together in masses, and learns its own strength. The interests and position of different trades become similar, because machinery tends to reduce wages to the same level, and to make less and less difference between the various kinds of labour. The increasing competition amongst the middle-class, and the commercial crises consequent thereupon, make wages always more variable, while the incessant improvements in machinery make the position of the Proletarians more and more uncertain, and the collisions between the individual workmen and the individual masters, assume more and more the character of collisions between two classes. The workmen commence to form trades-unions against the masters; they turn out, to prevent threatened reductions in their wages. They form associations to help each other in, and to provision themselves for, these occasional revolts. Here and there the struggle takes the form of riots.

From time to time the Proletarians are, for a moment, victorious, yet the result of their struggle is not an immediate advantage, but the ever increasing union amongst their class. This union is favoured by the facility of communication under the modern industrial system, whereby the Proletarians belonging to the remotest localities are placed in connection with each other. But connection is all that is wanting to change innumerable local struggles, having all the same character, into one national struggle—into a battle of classes. Every battle between different classes is a political battle, and the union, which it took the burghers of the middle ages centuries to bring about, by means of their few and awkward roads, can be accomplished in a few years by the modern Proletarians, by means of railways and steamships. This organisation of the Proletarians into a class, and therewith into a political party, is incessantly destroyed by the competitive principle. Yet it always reappears, and each time it is stronger and more extensive. It compels the legal acknowledgment of detached Proletarian rights, by profiting of the divisions in the bourgeois camp. For example, the Ten Hours Bill in England. The struggles of the ruling classes amongst themselves are favourable to the development of the Proletariat. The middle-class has always been in a state of perpetual warfare—first, against the aristocracy; and then against that part of itself whose interests are opposed to the further evolution of the industrial system; and, thirdly, against the bourgeoisie of other countries. During all of these battles, the middle-class has ever been obliged to appeal for help to the Proletarians, and so to draw the latter into the political movement. This class, therefore, has armed the Proletarians against itself, by letting them share in its own means of cultivation. Further, as we have already seen, the evolution of the industrial system has thrown a large portion of the ruling class into the ranks of the Proletarians, or at least rendered the means of subsistence very precarious for this portion. A new element of progress for the Proletariat. Finally, as the settlement of the class-struggle draws near, the process of dissolution goes on so rapidly within the ruling-class—within the worn-out body politic—that a small fraction of this class separates from it, and joins the revolutionary class, in whose hands lies the future. In the earlier revolutions a part of the noblesse joined the bourgeoisie, in the present one, a part of the bourgeoisie is joining the Proletariat, and particularly a part of the Bourgeois-ideologists, or middle-class thinkers, who have attained a theoretical knowledge of the whole historical movement.

The Proletariat is the only truly revolutionary Class amongst the present enemies of the Bourgeoisie. All the other classes of Society are being destroyed by the modern industrial system, the Proletariat is its peculiar product. The small manufacturers, shopkeepers, proprietors, peasants, etc., all fight against the Bourgeoisie, in order to defend their position as small Capitalists. They are, therefore, not revolutionary, but conservative. They are even reactionary, for they attempt to turn backwards the chariot wheels of History. When these subordinate classes are revolutionary, they are so with reference to their necessary absorption into the Proletariat; they defend their future, not their present, interests—they leave their own Class point of view to take up that of the Proletariat.

The Mob—this product of the decomposition of the lowest substrata of the old Social system—is partly forced into the revolutionary Proletarian movement. The social position of this portion of the people makes it, however, in general a ready and venal tool for Reactionist intrigues.

The vital conditions of Society, as at present constituted, no longer exist for the Proletariat. Its very existence is a flagrant contradiction to those conditions. The Proletarian has no property; the relation in which he stands to his family has nothing in common with Middle-class family relationships; the modern system of industrial labour, the modern slavery of Labour under Capital, which obtains in England as in France, in America as in Germany, has robbed him of his National Character. Law, Morality, Religion, are for him so many Middle-class prejudices, under which so many Middle-class interests are concealed. All the hitherto dominant Classes, have tried to preserve the position they had already attained, by imposing the conditions under which they possessed and increased their possessions, upon the rest of Society. But the Proletarians can gain possession of the Productive power of Society—of the instruments of Labour—only by annihilating their own, hitherto acknowledged mode of appropriation. The Proletarians have nothing of their own to secure, their task is to destroy all previously existing private securities and possessions. All the historical movements hitherto recorded were the movements of minorities, or movements in the interest of minorities. The Proletarian movement is the independent movement of the immense majority in favour of the immense majority. The Proletariat, the lowest stratum of existing society, cannot arouse, cannot rise without causing the complete disruption and dislocation of all the superincumbent classes. Though the struggle of the Proletariat against the Bourgeoisie is not a National struggle in its Content—or Reality—it is so in its Form. The Proletarians of every country must settle accounts with the Bourgeoisie there.

While we have thus sketched the general aspect presented by the development of the Proletariat, we have followed the more or less concealed Civil War pervading existing Society, to the point where it must break forth in an open Revolution, and where the Proletarians arrive at the supremacy of their own class through the violent fall of the Bourgeoisie. We have seen that all previous forms of Society have rested upon the antagonism of oppressing and oppressed Classes. But in order to oppress a Class, the conditions under which it can continue at least its enslaved existence must be secured. The Serf in the Middle Ages, even within his serfdom, could better his condition and become a member of the Commune; the burghers could become a Middle-class under the yoke of feudal Monarchy. But the modern Proletarian, instead of improving his condition with the development of modern Industry, is daily sinking deeper and deeper even below the conditions of existence of his own Class. The Proletarian tends to become a pauper, and Pauperism is more rapidly developed than population and Wealth. From this it appears, that the Middle-class is incapable of remaining any longer the ruling Class of Society, and of compelling Society to adopt the conditions of Middle-class existence as its own vital conditions. This Class is incapable of governing, because it is incapable of ensuring the bare existence of its Slaves, even within the limits of their slavery, because it is obliged to keep them, instead of being kept by them. Society can no longer exist under this Class, that is, its existence is no longer compatible with that of Society. The most indispensable condition for the existence and supremacy of the Bourgeoisie is the accumulation of Wealth in the hands of private individuals, the formation and increase of Capital.

The condition upon which Capital depends is the Wages-system, and this system again, is founded upon the Competition of the Proletarians with each other. But the progress of the modern industrial system, towards which the Bourgeoisie lend an unconscious and involuntary support, tends to supersede the isolated position of Proletarians by the revolutionary Union of their Class, and to replace Competition by Association. The progress of the modern industrial system, therefore, cuts away, from under the feet of the Middle-class, the very ground upon which they produce and appropriate to themselves the produce of Labour. Thus the Bourgeoisie produce before all the men who dig their very grave. Their destruction and the victory of the Proletarians are alike unavoidable.

Chapter two: proletarians and communists

What relationship subsists between the Communists and the Proletarians?—The Communists form no separate party in opposition to the other existing working-class parties. They have no interest different from that of the whole Proletariat. They lay down no particular principles according to which they wish to direct and to shape the Proletarian movement. The Communists are distinguishable among the various sections of the Proletarian party on two accounts—namely, that in the different national Proletarian struggles, the Communists understand, and direct attention to, the common interest of the collective Proletariat, an interest independent of all nationality; and that, throughout the various phases of development assumed by the struggle between the Bourgeoisie and the Proletariat, the Communists always represent the interest of the Whole Movement. In a word, the Communists are the most advanced, the most progressive section, among the Proletarian parties of all countries; and this section has a theoretical advantage, compared with the bulk of the Proletariat—it has obtained an insight into the historical conditions, the march, and the general results of the Proletarian Movement. The more immediate aim of the Communists is that of all other Proletarian sections. The organisation of the Proletariat as a class, the destruction of Middle-class supremacy, and the conquest of political power by the Proletarians.

The theoretical propositions of the Communists are not based upon Ideas, or Principles, discovered by this or that Universal Reformer. Their propositions are merely general expressions for the actual conditions, causes, etc., of an existing battle between certain classes, the conditions of an historical Movement which is going on before our very eyes.

The abolition of existing conditions of Property does not form a distinguishing characteristic of Communism. All such conditions have been subject to a continual change, to the operation of many historical Movements. The French Revolution, for example, destroyed the feudal conditions of property, and replaced them by Bourgeois ones. It is not, therefore, the abolition of property generally which distinguishes Communism; it is the abolition of Bourgeois property. But Modern Middle-class private property is the last and most perfect expression for that mode of Production and Distribution which rests on the antagonism of classes, on the using up of the many by the few. In this sense, indeed, the Communists might resume their whole Theory in that single expression—The abolition of private property.

It has been reproached to us, the Communists, that we wish to destroy the property which is the product of a man's own labour; self-acquired property, the basis of all personal freedom, activity, and independence. Self-acquired property! Do you mean the property of the small shopkeeper, small tradesman, small peasant, which precedes the present system of Middle-class property? We do not need to abolish that, the progress of industrial development is daily destroying it. Or do you mean modern Middle-class property? Does labour under the Wages-system create property for the Wages-slave, for the Proletarian? No. It creates Capital, that is, a species of property which plunders Wages-labour, for Capital can only increase on condition of creating a new supply of Wages-labour, in order to use it up anew. Property, in its present form, rests upon the antagonism of Capital and Wages-labour. Let us look at both sides of this antithesis. To be a Capitalist means to occupy not only a personal, but a social position in the system of production.

Capital is a collective product, and can be used and set in motion only by the common activity of many, or, to speak exactly, only by the united exertions of all the members of society. Capital is thus not an individual, it is a social power. Therefore, when Capital is changed into property belonging in common to all the members of society, personal property is not thereby changed into social property. It was social property before. The social character only of property, in such a case, is changed. Property loses its class character.

Let us now turn to Wages-labour.

The minimum rate of wages is the average price of Proletarian labour. And what is the minimum rate of wages? It is that quantity of produce which is necessary to conserve the working capacities of the labourer. What the Wages-slave can gain by his activity is merely what is requisite for the bare reproduction of his existence. We by no means wish to abolish this personal appropriation of the products of labour, an appropriation leaving no net profit, no surplus, to be applied to command the labour of others. We only wish to change the miserably insufficient character of this appropriation, whereby the producer lives only to increase Capital; that is, whereby he is kept alive only so far as it may be the interest of the ruling class.

In Middle-class society, actual living labour is nothing but a means of increasing accumulated labour. In Communistic society, accumulated labour is only a means of enlarging, increasing, and varifying the vital process of the producers. In Middle-class society, the Past reigns over the Present. In Communistic society, the Present reigns over the Past. In Middle-class society, Capital is independent and personal, while the active individual is dependent and deprived of personality. And the destruction of such a system is called by Middle-class advocates, the destruction of personality and freedom. They are so far right, that the question in hand is the destruction of Middle-class personality, independence, and freedom.

Within the present Middle-class conditions of production, freedom means free trade, freedom of buying and selling. But if trade, altogether, is to fall, so will free trade fall with the rest. The declamations about free trade, as all the remaining Bourgeois declamations upon the subject of freedom generally, have a meaning only when opposed to fettered trade, and to the enslaved tradesmen of the Middle Ages; they have no meaning whatever in reference to the Communistic destruction of profit-mongering, of the Middle-class conditions of production, and of the Middle-class itself.

You are horrified that we aim at the abolition of private property. But under your present system of society, private property has no existence for nine-tenths of its members; its existence is based upon the very fact that it exists not at all for nine-tenths of the population. You reproach us, then, that we aim at the abolition of a species of property which involves, as a necessary condition, the absence of all property for the immense majority of society. In a word, you reproach us that we aim at the destruction of YOUR property. That is precisely what we aim at.

From the moment when Labour can no longer be changed into Capital—into money, or rent—into a social power capable of being monopolised, that is, from the moment when personal property can no longer constitute itself as Middle-class property, from that moment you declare that human personality is abolished. You acknowledge, then, that for you personality generally means the personality of the Bourgeois, the Middle-class proprietor. It is precisely this kind of personality which is to be destroyed. Communism deprives no one of the right of appropriating social products; it only takes away from him the power of appropriating the command over the labour of others.

It has been objected that activity will cease, and a universal laziness pervade society, were the abolition of private property once accomplished. According to this view of the matter, Middle-class society ought, long since, to have been ruined through idleness; for under the present system, those who do work acquire no property, and those who acquire property do no work. This objection rests upon the tautological proposition, that there will be no Wages-labour whenever there is no Capital.

All the objections made to the Communistic mode of producing and distributing physical products have also been directed against the production and distribution of intellectual products. As, in the opinion of the Bourgeois, the destruction of class property involves the cessation of appropriation, in like manner the cessation of class-civilisation, in his opinion, is identical with the cessation of civilisation generally. The civilisation whose loss he deplores, is the system of civilising men into machines.

But do not dispute with us, while you measure the proposed abolition of Middle-class property, by your Middle-class ideas of freedom, civilisation, jurisprudence, and the like. Your ideas are the necessary consequences of the Middle-class conditions of property and production, as your jurisprudence is the Will of your class raised to the dignity of Law, a Will whose subject is given in the economical conditions of your class. The selfish mode of viewing the question, whereby you confound your transitory conditions of production and property with the eternal laws of Reason and Nature, is common to all ruling classes. What you understand with regard to Antique and Feudal property, you cannot understand with regard to modern Middle-class property. The destruction of domestic ties! Even the greatest Radicals are shocked at this scandalous intention of the Communists.

Upon what rests the present system, the Bourgeois system of family relationships? Upon Capital, upon private gains, on profit-mongering. In its most perfect form it exists only for the Bourgeoisie, and it finds a befitting compliment in the compulsory celibacy of the Proletarians, and in public prostitution. The Bourgeois family system naturally disappears with the disappearance of its complement, and the destruction of both is involved in the destruction of Capital. Do you reproach us that we intend abolishing the using up of children by their parents? We acknowledge this crime. Or that we will abolish the most endearing relationships, by substituting a public and social system of education for the existing private one? And is not your system of education also determined by society? By the social conditions, within the limits of which you educate? By the more or less direct influence of society, through the medium of your schools, and so forth? The Communists do not invent the influence of society upon education; they only seek to change its character, to rescue education from the influence of a ruling class. Middle-class talk about domestic ties and education, about the endearing connection of parent and child, becomes more and more disgusting in proportion as the family ties of the Proletarians are torn asunder, and their children changed into machines, into articles of commerce, by the extension of the modern industrial system.

But you intend introducing a community of women, shrieks the whole Middle-class like a tragic chorus. The Bourgeois looks upon his wife as a mere instrument of production; he is told that the instruments of production are to be used up in common, and thus he naturally supposes that women will share the common fate of other machines. He does not even dream that it is intended, on the contrary, to abolish the position of woman as a mere instrument of production. For the rest, nothing can be more ludicrous than the highly moral and religious horror entertained by the Bourgeoisie towards the pretended official community of women among the Communists. We do not require to introduce community of women, it has always existed. Your Middle-class gentry are not satisfied with having the wives and daughters of their Wages-slaves at their disposal—not to mention the innumerable public prostitutes—but they take a particular pleasure in seducing each other's wives. Middle-class marriage is in reality a community of wives. At the most, then, we could only be reproached for wishing to substitute an open, above-board community of women, for the present mean, hypocritical, sneaking kind of community. But it is evident enough that with the disappearance of the present conditions of production, the community of women occasioned by them—namely, official and non-official prostitution will also disappear.

The Communists are further reproached with desiring to destroy patriotism, the feeling of Nationality.

The Proletarian has no Fatherland. You cannot deprive him of that which he has not got. When the Proletariat obtains political supremacy, becomes the National Class, and constitutes itself as the Nation—it will, indeed, be national, though not in the middle-class sense of the word. The National divisions and antagonisms presented by the European Nations, already tend towards obliteration through the development of the Bourgeoisie, through the influence of free-trade, a worldwide market, the uniformity of the modern modes of Production and the conditions of modern life arising out of the present industrial system.

The supremacy of the Proletariat will hasten this obliteration of national peculiarities, for the united action of—at least—all civilized countries is one of the first conditions of Proletarian emancipation. In proportion to the cessation of the using up of one individual by an other, will be the cessation of the using up of one nation by another. The hostile attitude assumed by nations towards each other will cease with the antagonisms of the classes into which each nation is divided.

The accusations against communism, which have been made from the Theological, Philosophical, and Ideological, points of view, deserve no further notice. Does it require any great degree of intellect to perceive that changes occur in our ideas, conceptions, and opinions, in a word, that the consciousness of man alters with every change in the conditions of his physical existence, in his social relations and position?

Does not the history of Ideas show, that intellectual production has always changed with the changes in material production? The ruling ideas of any age have always been the ideas of the then ruling class. You talk of ideas which have revolutionised society; but you merely express the fact, that within the old form of society, the elements of a new one were being formed, and that the dissolution of the old ideas was keeping pace with the dissolution of the old conditions of social life.

When the antique world was in its last agony, Christianity triumphed over the antique religion. When the dogmas of Christianity were superseded by the enlightenment of the eighteenth century, feudal society was concentrating its last efforts against the then revolutionary Bourgeoisie. The ideas of religious liberty and freedom of thought were the expressions of unlimited competition in the affairs and free trade in the sphere of intellect and religion. But, you say, theological, moral, philosophical, political and legal ideas, are subject to be modified by the progress of historical development. Religion, ethics, philosophy, politics, and jurisprudence are, however, of all times. And we find, besides certain eternal ideas, for example, Freedom, Justice, and the like—which are common to all the various social phases and states. But communism destroys these eternal truths; it pretends to abolish religion and Ethics, instead of merely giving them a new form; Communism, therefore, contradicts all preceding modes of historical development. To what does this accusation amount? The history of all preceding states of society is simply the history of class antagonisms, which were fought under different conditions, and assumed different forms during the different historical epochs. Whatever form these antagonisms may have assumed, the using up of one part of society by another part, is a fact, common to the whole past. No wonder then, that the social consciousness of past ages should have a common ground, in spite of the multiplicity and diversity of social arrangements: that it should move in certain common forms of thinking, which will completely disappear with the disappearance of class antagonism. The communistic revolution is the most thorough-going rupture with the traditionary conditions of property, no wonder then, that its progress will involve the completest rupture with traditionary ideas.

But we must have done with the middle-class accusations against communism.

We have seen that the first step in the proletarian revolution will be the conquest of Democracy, the elevation of the Proletariat to the state of the ruling class. The Proletarians will use their political supremacy in order to deprive the middle-class of the command of capital; to centralise all the instruments of production in the hands of the State, that is, in those of the whole proletariat organized as the ruling class, and to increase the mass of productive power with the utmost possible rapidity. It is a matter of course that this can be done, at first, only by despotic interference with the rights of property, and middle-class conditions of production. By regulations, in fact, which—economically considered—appear insufficient and untenable; which, therefore, in the course of the revolution, necessitate ulterior and more radical measures, and are unavoidable as a means towards a thorough change in the modes of production. These regulations will, of course, be different in different countries. But for the most advanced countries, the following will be pretty generally applicable:

1) The national appropriation of the land, and the application of rent to the public revenue.
2) A heavy progressive tax.
3) Abolition of the right of inheritance.
4) Confiscation of the property of all emigrants and rebels.
5) Centralization of credit in the hands of the State, by means of a national bank, with an exclusive monopoly and a state-capital.
6) Centralization of all the means of communication in the hands of the state.
7) Increase of the national manufactories; of the instruments of production; the cultivation of waste lands and the improvement of the land generally according to a common plan.
8) Labour made compulsory for all; and the organisation of industrial armies, especially for agriculture.
9) The union of manufacturing and agricultural industry; with a view of gradually abolishing the antagonism between town and country.
10) The public and gratuitous education of all children; the abolition of the present system of factory labour for children; the conjunction of education and material production with other regulations of a similar nature.

When Class distinctions will have finally disappeared, and production will have been concentrated in the hands of this Association which comprises the whole nation, the public power will lose its political character. Political power in the exact sense of the word, being the organised power of one class, which enables it to oppress another. When the proletariat has been forced to unite as a class during its struggle with the Bourgeoisie, when it has become the ruling class by a revolution, and as such has destroyed, by force, the old conditions of production, it destroys, necessarily, with these conditions of production, the conditions of existence of all class antagonism, of classes generally, and thus it destroys, also, its own supremacy as a class. The old Bourgeois Society, with its classes, and class antagonisms, will be replaced by an association, wherein the free development of EACH is the condition of the free development of ALL.

Chapter three: socialist and communist literature

I. Reactionary socialism
a. Feudal socialism.

The historical position of the French and English Aristocracy devolved upon them, at a certain period, the task of writing pamphlets against the social system of the modern Bourgeoisie. These Aristocracies were again beaten by a set of detestable parvenus and nobodies in the July Days of 1830, and in the English Reform Bill movement. There could be no longer any question about a serious political struggle. There remained only the possibility of conducting a literary combat. But even in the territory of Literature, the old modes of speech, current during the Restoration, had become impossible. In order to excite sympathy, the Aristocracy had to assume the semblance of disinterestedness, and to draw up their accusation of the Bourgeoisie, apparently as advocates for the used-up Proletarians. The Aristocracy thus revenged themselves on their new masters—by lampoons and fearful prophecies of coming woe. In this way feudal socialism arose—half lamentation, half libel, half echo of the Past, half prophecy of a threatening Future—sometimes striking the very heart of the Bourgeoisie by its sarcastic, bitter judgments, but always accompanied by a certain tinge of the ludicrous, from its complete inability to comprehend the march of modern history. The Feudal Socialists waved the Proletarian alms-bag aloft, to assemble the people around them. But as often as the people came, they perceived upon the hind parts of these worthies, the old feudal arms and quarterings, and abandoned them with noisy and irreverent hilarity. A part of the French Legitimists and the party of Young England played this farce.

When the Feudalists show that their mode of exploitation (using up one class by another) was different from the Bourgeois mode, they forget that their mode was practicable only under circumstances and conditions which have passed away—never to return. When they show that the modern Proletariat never existed under their supremacy, they simply forget, that the modern Bourgeoisie is the necessary offspring of their own social order. For the rest, they so little conceal the reactionary nature of their criticism, that their chief reproach against the Bourgeois-regime is that of having created a class which is destined to annihilate the old social forms and arrangements altogether. It is not so much that the Bourgeoisie created a Proletariat, but that this Proletariat is revolutionary. Hence, in their political practice, they take part in all reactionary measures against the working classes; and in ordinary life, despite their grandiloquent phrases, they condescend to gather the golden apples, and to give up chivalry, true love, and honour for the traffic in wool, butcher's meat, and corn. As the parson has always gone hand-in-hand with the landlord, so has Priestly Socialism with Feudal Socialism. Nothing is easier than to give Christian asceticism a tinge of Socialism. Has not Christianity itself vociferated against private property, marriage, and the powers that be? Have not charity, and mendicity, celibacy and mortification of the flesh, monastic life, and the supremacy of the Church been held up in the place of these things? Sacred Socialism is merely the holy water, with which the priest besprinkles the impotent wrath of the Aristocracy.

b. Shopocrat-socialism.[1]

The Feudal Aristocracy are not the only class who are, or will be, destroyed by the Bourgeoisie. Not the only class, the conditions of whose existence become exhausted and disappear, under the modern middle-class system. The mediaeval burgesses and yeoman were the precursors of the modern middle-class. In countries possessing a small degree of industrial and commercial development, this intermediate class still vegetates side by side with the nourishing Bourgeoisie. In countries where modern civilization has been developed, a new intermediate class has been formed; floating as it were, between the Bourgeoisie and the Proletariat; and always renewing itself as a component part of Bourgeois society. Yet, the persons belonging to this class are con-

---

1. The term in the original is Kleinburger, meaning small burghers, or citizens. A class comprising small capitalists generally, whether small farmers, small manufacturers, or retail shopkeepers. As these last form the predominant element of this class in England, I have chosen the term Shopocrat to express the German term. [HM footnote]

stantly forced by competition downwards into the Proletariat, and the development of the modern industrial system will bring about the time when this small capitalist class will entirely disappear, and be replaced by managers and stewards, in commerce, manufactures, and agriculture. In countries like France, where far more than one half of the population are small freeholders, it was natural that writers who took part with the Proletariat against the Bourgeoisie, should measure the Bourgeois-regime by the small-capitalist standard; and should envisage the Proletarian question from the small-capitalist point of view. In this way arose the system of Shopocrat Socialism. Sismondi is the head of this school, in England as well as in France. This school of socialism has dissected with great acuteness the modern system of production, and exposed the fallacies contained therein. It unveiled the hypocritical evasions of the political economists. It irrefutably demonstrated the destructive effects of machinery, and the division of labour; the concentration of capital and land in a few hands; over-production; commercial crisis; the necessary destruction of the small capitalist; the misery of the Proletariat; anarchy in production, and scandalous inequality in the distribution of wealth; the destructive industrial wars of one nation with another; and the disappearance of old manners and customs, of patriarchal family arrangements, and of old nationalities. But in its practical application, this Shopocrat, or Small-Capitalist Socialism, wishes either to re-establish the old modes of production and traffic, and with these, the old conditions of property, and old society altogether—or forcibly to confine the modern means of production and traffic within the limits of these antique conditions of property, which were actually destroyed, necessarily so, by these very means. In both cases, Shopocrat Socialism is, at the same time reactionary and Utopian. Corporations and guilds in manufactures, patriarchal idyllic arrangements in agriculture, are its beau ideal. This kind of Socialism has run to seed, and exhausted itself in silly lamentations over the past.

c. German—or 'true' socialism[1]

The Socialist and Communist literature of France originated under the Bourgeois-regime, and was the literary expression of the

---

1. It was the set of writers characterised in the following chapter, who themselves called their theory 'TRUE SOCIALISM'. If, therefore, after

struggle against middle-class supremacy. It was introduced into Germany at a time when the Bourgeoisie there had began their battle against Feudal despotism.

German Philosophers—half-philosophers, and would-be literati—eagerly seized on this literature, and forgot that with the immigration of these French writings into Germany, the advanced state of French society, and of French class-struggles, had not, as a matter of course, immigrated along with them. This French literature, when brought into contact with the German phases of social development, lost all its immediate practical significance, and assumed a purely literary aspect. It could appear in no other way than as an idle speculation upon the best possible state of society, upon the realization of the true nature of man. In a similar manner, the German philosophers of the 18th century considered the demands of the first French Revolution as the demands of "Practical Reason" in its general sense, and the will of the revolutionary French bourgeoisie was for them the law of the pure will, of volition as it ought to be; the law of man's inward nature. The all-engrossing problem for the German literati was to bring the new French ideas into accordance with their old philosophic conscience; or rather, to appropriate the French ideas without leaving the philosophic point of view. This appropriation took place in the same way as one masters a foreign language; namely, by translation. It is known how the Monks of the middle-ages treated the manuscripts of the Greek and Roman classics. They wrote silly Catholic legends over the original text. The German literati did the very reverse, with respect to the profane French literature. They wrote their philosophical nonsense behind the French original. For example, behind the French critique of the modern money-system, they wrote "Estrangement of Human Nature"; behind the French critique of the bourgeois-regime, they wrote, "Destruction of the Supremacy of the Absolute", and so forth. They baptized this interpolation of their philosophic modes of speech, with the French ideas by various names; 'Philosophy in Action', 'True Socialism', 'The German Philosophy of Socialism', 'Philosophical Foundation of Socialism', and the like.

---

perusing this chapter, the reader should not agree with them as to the name, this is no fault of the authors of the manifesto. [HM footnote]

The socialist and communist literature of France was completely emasculated. And when it had ceased, in German hands, to express the struggle of one class against another, the Germans imagined they had overcome French one-sidedness. They imagined they represented, not true interests and wants, but the interests and wants of abstract truth; not the proletarian interest, but the interest of human nature, as man as belonging to no class, a native of no merely terrestrial countries—of man, belonging of the misty, remote region of philosophical imagination.

This German socialism, which composed its clumsy school themes with such exemplary solemnity, and then cried them along the street, gradually lost its pedantic and primitive innocence. The battle of the German, particularly of the Prussian, bourgeoisie against feudalism and absolute monarchy, in a word, the liberal movement, became more serious. True socialism had now the desired opportunity of placing socialist demands in opposition to the actual political movement; of hurling the traditionary second-hand Anathemas against liberalism, constitutional governments, bourgeois competition and free trade, bourgeois freedom of the press, bourgeois juries, bourgeois freedom and equality; the opportunity of preaching to the masses that they had nothing to gain and everything to lose by this middle-class movement. German socialism forgot, very opportunely, that the French polemics, whose unmeaning echo it was—presupposed the modern middle-class system of society, with the corresponding physical conditions of social existence, and a suitable political constitution presupposed, in fact, the very things which had no existence in Germany, and which were the very things to be obtained by the middle-class movement. German socialism was used by the German despots and their followers—priests, schoolmasters, bureaucrats and bullfrog country squires—as a scarecrow to frighten the revolutionary middle-class. It was the agreeable finish to the grapeshot and cat o' nine tails, with which these Governments replied to the first proletarian insurrections of Germany. While "true socialism" was thus employed in assisting the Governments against the German bourgeoisie, it also directly represented a reactionary interest, that of the German small capitalists and shopocracy. In Germany the real social foundation of the existing state of things was this class, remaining since the 16th century, and always renewing itself under slightly different forms.

Its preservation was the preservation of the existing order of things in Germany. The industrial and political supremacy of the bourgeoisie involved the annihilation of this intermediate class; on the one hand, by the centralisation of capital; on the other, by the creation of a revolutionary proletariat. German, or "true" socialism, appeared to this shopocracy as a means of killing two birds with one stone. It spread like an epidemic. The robe of speculative cobwebs, adorned with rhetorical flourishes and sickly sentimentalism—in which the German socialists wrapped the dry bones of their eternal, absolute truths, increased the demand for their commodity among this public. And the German socialists were not wanting in due appreciation of their mission, to be the grandiloquent representatives of the German shopocrats. They proclaimed the German nation to be the archetypal nation; the German cockneys to be archetypal men. They gave every piece of cockney rascality a hidden socialist sense, whereby it was interpreted to mean the reverse of rascality. They reached the limits of their system when they directly opposed the destructive tendency of communism, and proclaimed their own sublime indifference towards all class-antagonism. With very few exceptions, all the so-called socialist and communist publications which circulate in Germany emanate from this school, and are enervating filthy trash.

II. Conservative, or bourgeois socialism

A part of the Bourgeoisie desires to alleviate social dissonances, with a view of securing the existence of middle-class society. To this section belong economists, philanthropists, humanitarians, improvers of the condition of the working classes, patrons of charitable institutions, cruelty-to-animals-bill supporters, temperance advocates, in a word, hole and corner reformers of the most varied and piebald aspect. This middle-class Socialism has even been developed into complete systems. As an example, we may cite Proudhon's Philosophy of Poverty. The socialist bourgeois wish to have the vital conditions of modern society without the accompanying struggles and dangers. They desire the existing order of things, minus the revolutionary and destructive element contained therein. They wish to have a bourgeoisie without a proletariat. The bourgeoisie, of course, consider the world wherein they reign, to be the best possible world. Bourgeois socialism develops this comfortable hypothesis into a complete system. When these socialists urge the proletariat to realise their system, to march towards the New Jerusalem, they ask, in reality, that the proletariat should remain within the limits of existing society, and yet lay aside all bitter and unfavourable opinions concerning it.

A second, less systematic, and more practical school of middle-class socialists try to hinder all revolutionary movements among the producers, by teaching them that their condition cannot be improved by this or that political change—but only by a change in the material conditions of life, in the economical arrangements of society. Yet, by a change in the modern life-conditions, these socialists do not mean the abolition of the middle-class modes of production and distribution, attainable only in a revolutionary manner, they mean administrative reforms, to be made within the limits of the old system, which, therefore, will leave the relation of capital and wages-labour untouched—and, at most, will merely simplify the details and diminish the cost of bourgeois government. This kind of socialism finds its most fitting expression in empty rhetorical flourishes. Free Trade! for the benefit of the working classes. A tariff! for the benefit of the working classes. Isolated imprisonment and the silent system! for the benefit of the working classes. This last phrase is the only sincere and earnest one, among the whole stock in trade of the middle-class socialists. Their socialism consists in affirming that the bourgeois is a bourgeois... for the benefit of the working classes!

III. Critical utopian socialiasm and communism

We do not speak here of the literature, which, in all the great revolutions of modern times, has expressed the demands of the proletariat: as leveller pamphleteers, the writings of Babeuf and others.[1]

The first attempts of the proletariat towards directly forwarding its own class-interest, made during the general movement which overthrew feudal society, necessarily failed—by reason of the crude, undeveloped form of the proletariat itself; as well as by the want of those material conditions for its emancipation, which are but the product of the bourgeois-epoch. The revolutionary literature, which accompanied this first movement of the

---

1. Marx and Engels' original refers to *"Babeuf and others"* but makes tno reference to the Levellers of the 17th century.

proletariat, had necessarily a reactionary content. It taught a universal asceticism and a rude sort of equality.

The Socialist and communist systems, properly so called, the systems of St. Simon, Owen, Fourier and others, originated in the early period of the struggle between the proletariat and the bourgeoisie, which we described in Chap. I. The inventors of these systems perceived the fact of class-antagonism, and the activity of the dissolvent elements within the prevailing social system. But they did not see any spontaneous historical action, any characteristic political movement, on the part of the proletariat. And because the development of class-antagonism keeps pace with the development of the industrial system, they could not find the material conditions for the emancipation of the proletariat; they were obliged to seek for a social science, for social laws, in order to create those conditions. Their personal inventive activity took the place of social activity, imaginary conditions of proletarian emancipation were substituted for the historical ones, and a subjective, fantastic organisation of society, for the gradual and progressive organisation of the proletariat as a class. The approaching phasis of universal history resolved itself, for them, into the propagandism and practical realisation of their peculiar social plans. They had, indeed, the consciousness of advocating the interest of the producers as the most suffering class of society. The proletariat existed for them, only under this point of view of the most oppressed class.

The undeveloped state of the class-struggle, and their own social position, induced these socialists to believe they were removed far above class-antagonism. They desired to improve the position of all the members of society, even of the most favoured. Hence, their continual appeals to the whole of society, even to the dominant class. You have only to understand their system, in order to see it is the best possible plan for the best possible state of society. Hence too, they reject all political, and particularly all revolutionary action, they desire to attain their object in a peaceful manner, and try to prepare the way for the new social gospel, by the force of example, by small, isolated experiments, which, of course, cannot but turn out signal failures.

This fantastic representation of future society expressed the feeling of a time when the proletariat was quite undeveloped, and had quite an imaginary conception of its own position—it was the expression of an instinctive want for a universal social revolution. There are, however, critical elements contained in all these socialist and communist writings. They attack the foundation of existing society. Hence they contain a treasure of materials for the enlightenment of the Producers. Their positive propositions regarding a future state of society; e.g. abolition of the antagonism of town and country, of family institutions, of individual accumulation, of wages-labour, the proclamation of social harmony, the change of political power into a mere superintendence of production—all these propositions expressed the abolition of class-antagonism, when this last was only commencing its evolution; and, therefore, they have, with these authors a purely Utopian sense.

The importance of critical-Utopian Socialism and Communism, stands in an inverted proportion to the progress of the historical movement. In proportion as the class-battle is evolved and assumes a definite form, so does this imaginary elevation over it, this fantastic resistance to it, lose all practical worth, all theoretical justification. Hence, it happens, that although the originators of these systems were revolutionary in various respects, yet their followers have invariably formed reactionary sects. They hold fast by their master's old dogmas and doctrines, in opposition to the progressive historical evolution of the Proletariat. They seek, therefore, logically enough, to deaden class opposition, to mediate between the extremes. They still dream of the experimental realization of their social Utopias through isolated efforts—the founding of a few *phalanstères*, of a few home colonies, of a small Icaria—a duodecimo edition of the New Jerusalem; and they appeal to the philanthropy of Bourgeois hearts and purses for the building expenses of these air-castles and chimeras. They gradually fall back into the category of the above mentioned reactionary or conservative Socialists, and distinguish themselves from these only by their more systematic pedantry, by their fanatical faith in the miraculous powers of their Social panacea. Hence, they violently oppose all political movements in the Proletariat, which indeed, can only be occasioned by a blind and wilful disbelief in the new Gospel. In France, the Fourierists oppose the Reformists; in England, the Owenites react against the Chartists.[1]

---

1. Macfarlane footnote: It is not to be forgotten that these lines were written before the revolution of February (1848), and that the examples have, accordingly, reference to the state of parties of that time.

Position of the communists in relation to the various existing opposition parties[1]

[Section II has made clear the relation of the Communists to the existing work class parties, such as the Chartists in England and the Social Reformers in America. The Communists fight for the attainment of the immediate aims, for the enforcement of the momentary interests of the working-class; but in the movement of the present, they also represent and take care of the future of that movement. In France, the Communists ally with the Social Democrats against the conservative and radical bourgeoisie, reserving, however, the right to take up a critical position in regard to phases and illusions traditionally handed down from the Great Revolution. In Switzerland, they support the Radicals, without losing sight of the fact that this party consists of antagonistic elements, partly of Democratic Socialists, in the French sense, partly of radical bourgeois. In Poland, they support the party that insists on an agrarian revolution as the prime condition for national emancipation, that party which fomented the insurrection of Krakow in 1846. In Germany, they fight with the bourgeoisie whenever it acts in a revolutionary way, against the absolute monarchy, the feudal squirearchy, and the petty-bourgeoisie. But they never cease, for a single instant, to instill into the working-class the clearest possible recognition of the hostile antagonism between bourgeoisie and proletariat, in order that the German workers may straightaway use, as so many weapons against the bourgeoisie, the social and political conditions that the bourgeoisie must necessarily introduce along with its supremacy, and in order that, after the fall of the reactionary classes in Germany, the fight against the bourgeoisie itself may

---

1. The text following, which appeared in the German edition, translated by Moore in 1888 - here bracketed - is omitted in this translation. Harney, as *Red Republican* editor, had reason to be wary of alerting the government to anything that might be seen as a 'conspiracy' hatched in London between 'aliens' and Chartists. He had, after all, as leader of the Fraternal Democrats, been party to talks during the year 1850 with the German Communists and French Blanquists about forming a 'World League of Revolutionary Socialists'. The Treason Felony Act of 1848 had already been used to prosecute—and transport to Van Dieman's Land—the Black London Chartist, William Cuffay, and the Irish revolutionary, John Mitchel.

immediately begin. The Communists turn their attention chiefly to Germany, because that country is on the eve of a bourgeois revolution that is bound to be carried out under more advanced conditions of European civilization and with a much more developed proletariat than that of England was in the seventeenth, and France in the eighteenth century, and because the bourgeois revolution in Germany will be but the prelude to an immediately following proletarian revolution.]

The Communists invariably support every revolutionary movement against the existing order of things, social and political. But in all these movements, they endeavour to point out the property question, whatever degree of development, in every particular case, it may have obtained—as the leading question. The Communists labour for the union and association of the revolutionary parties of all countries. The Communists disdain to conceal their opinions and ends. They openly declare that these ends can be attained only by the overthrow of all hitherto existing social arrangements. Let the ruling classes tremble at a Communist Revolution. The Proletarians have nothing to lose in it save their chains. They will gain a World. Let the Proletarians of all countries unite!

Index

Althusser, Louis xi
America
 land question 97
 slavery 2, 48, 97
 women's oppression 48
Anaxagoras xv
Anthony, Mark 29
Anti-Corn Law League 21, 34, 63, 69
Antigone v
Archimedes 46
Aristotle 13
Arthur, Liz vi, vii, viii
Lord Ashley, Earl of Shaftesbury xxii, 45, 97
Athanasius of Alexandria 99
Athens 12
Austen, Jane vi, viii
Australia 53
Austria 52

Baldwin 3
Bannockburn vii
Baudelaire, Charles 6
Bedlam 60
Bentham, Jeremy
 Book of Fallacies xxiii
Berman, Marshall
 on Goethe and Saint-Simon 46
Bermuda Islands 47
Bible Society 95
Black, David
 Helen Macfarlane: A Feminist, Revolutionary Journalist and Philosopher in Mid-19th Century England vi
Blanc, Louis xxvii, xxviii, 18
Blanquists xxvi
Blanqui, ugust 109
Blomfield, Charles 104–110
Blum, Robert 87
Borgia, Cæsar 27
Bradford 50
Bright, John 21, 24, 41, 48, 50, 59, 69, 71, 87
British Constitution 5, 14, 29–46, 52

Buddha 30
Burns, Mary and Lizzie xxx
Byron, Lord George ii
 Don Juan 60

Caesar, Julius 4, 14, 29
calico printing vii–viii
Carlyle, Thomas ix, x, 1–22, 73, 105
caste 17
Central European Democratic Committee xxvii
Cervantes, Miguel de x
charity 94
Charles the Tenth 20
Charlston, David i
Chartism ix, xxviii, 88
 1839 Convention ix
 Kennington Common demonstration ix
 Land Plan xxix, 23
 National Charter Association 37, 44–46
 National Charter League 24
 People's Charter (Six Points) 37, 44, 50
 Social Reform League 44
 Tract Fund 46
chattels 12
Christian Socialism 55
Christ, Jesus iii, 5, 8, 9, 13, 18, 21, 22, 56
Church of England xxxi, 5, 14–16, 27, 38, 41, 88, 89, 98, 103–110
Church of Scotland 16
Cicero, Marcus Tullius 13
Clark, Thomas 23, 24
classes 77
Clydeside viii
Cobbett, William 61
Cobden, Richard 21, 26, 41, 48, 50, 52, 59, 69, 71–78, 87
Coleridge, Samuel Taylor i
common land xxvi
Communist League xxvi

Communist Manifesto ii, x, xxii–xxvi, 84, 119–148
  "the most revolutionary document ever given to the world" x
constitution. *See* British Constitution
Council of Trent 106
Cox, Sir Richard 14
Crimean War 71
Currency Bill 63

Dagon 11
Dawson, George 28
Debord, Guy xxiv
democracy 2–22
  "the nightmare and old bogy" xxiii
Democratic Review of British Politics iii, x, 27
Demuth, Helene xxviii
Descartes, René xiii, xv
The Destructive 2
dialectics xi
Dickens, Charles x, 50, 51, 53, 54, 91
Don Quixote 26
Dorset 96–97
Duke of Wellington 40
Dunyaevskaya, Raya v
Dupont, Pierre 6

Edward I 32
Edwards, Herbert and Walter xxxii
Edwards, John Wilkinson xxxi
egoistic desire i
Egypt 34
Einstein, Albert xi
El Dorado 10
Eliot, George ii, xxii, xxxi, 55
Ellis, Sarah Stickney 83
Emerson, Ralph Waldo xxiii, 14, 21, 22
Engels, Friedrich x, xvii, xxvi, xxxi. *See also Communist Manifesto*
  on Saint-Simon 45
Enlightenment xii, xvi
Evans, George Henry 97
Evans, Marian. *See* Eliot, George

Farmers Wool League 33
feminism 48
Ferrand, William Busfeild 33

Feuerbach, Ludwig xviii, xxxi, 55
  Essence of Christianity xvii–xviii
Fichte, Johann Gottlieb xiv
Flodden vii
Fox, William Johnson 16
France 72
Frankfurt 71, 76
Fraternal Democrats xxvi, xxviii, 68
Frederick, Karl 55
freedom 8
Freiligrath, Ferdinand 55
French Revolution iii, xii
Friend of the People i, xxviii

George III 30
German Idealism i–ii, xv–xx, 5, 7, 8, 13, 55, 107
Geronimo Black 10
Glasgow vi, viii
Goethe, Johann Wolfgang von 1, 46
  mockery of God 108
Gooch, Sir Daniel 95
Gotham, Wise men of 8, 50
Graham, Sir James 40
Great Exhibition 50, 60
Gregory the Great 103
Grey, Sir George 40

Habsburg Monarchy ix
Hallam, Henry 30
Harney, George Julian iii, ix, xxvi–xxix, 23, 57
  'Mr Hippipharra' xxvii
Harney, Mary xxviii–xxix
Haynau, Baron von 4, 10, 79–82
Hebe 10
Hegel, George Wilhelm Friedrich xi–xii, xiv–xix, 7
  and Helen Macfarlane ii–iv, 11–12
  and Kojève iii
  'old mole' 37
  on Sophocles' Antigone 84
  Phenomenology of Spirit xxii
  Philosophy of Religion xv
Heine, Heinrich x, xiii
  'The New Pantheism' 110
Henderson, Lizanne and Cowan, Edward
  Scottish Fairy Belief: A History xxv

Heraclitus 26
Herbert, Sidney 54
Hercules 10
Hetherington, Henry 2
Hindoo religion 17
History and Literature iii, x
hobgoblin
  concept xxii–xxvi
  demotic curses on common land xxiii, xxv
Hölderlin, Friedrich xiv
Holloway, Richard vi
Homer x, 10
Hudson, George 63
Hume, David 32
  An Inquiry Concerning Human Understanding xii
Hume, Joseph 24
Hunt, Thornton Leigh 55

India 34
International Congress of the Friends of Peace 71–78
Ireland 73, 85, 92, 97

James II 30
Jones, Ernst 57, 104
Joseph, Franz 4

Kant, Immanuel xii–xiv
Kenny Process Team xxiv
King of Sardinia 52
Kingsley, Charles 55
Knowledge Tax. *See* Stamp Duty
Kojève, Alexandre iii

Lamartine, Alphonse de x, 91–95
The Leader 55
Lennox, General Charles Gordon (Duke of Richmond) 33
Lewes, George Henry 55
Liebig, Justus viii
Linebaugh, Peter xxv
Lollards 7
Luther, Martin 7, 56
Luxemberg, Rosa v

Macaulay, Thomas Babington 30
Macfarlane, Agnes xxx

Macfarlane, George (father) vii
Macfarlane, Helen
  BBC Radio Scotland, 'Women With a Past' vi–ix
  born vi
  Communist Manifesto translation x
  died xxxii
  emigrates xxx–xxxii
  and Hegel 11–12
  'Howard Morton' x
  maries Francis Proust xxix
  marries John Wilkinson Edwards xxxi
Macfarlane, John xxix
Macfarlane, William Stenhouse viii
Machiavelli, Niccolò di Bernardo dei 27
Magna Carta 30
Mainz 1
Malthus, Thomas 26, 72
Manchester School x, 23, 26, 34, 60, 61
Marat, Jean-Paul
  Friend of the People iii
Marcuse, Herbert xx
Marx, Heinrich xxvii
Marx, Jenny xxvi
Marx, Karl x, xxvi. *See also Communist Manifesto*
  on ad hominem 9
  Capital viii
  'Critique of Hegel's Philosophy of Right: Introduction' xxi
  'old mole' 38
  'revolution in permanence' xxvi
  "the muck of ages" 57
  "weapon of criticism" 9
Mazzini, Guiseppe xxvii
Melville, Herman v
Metternich, Klemens von 4
Milton, John x, 79
monism xiii
Moore, Samuel ii
More, Sir Thomas 33
Morison, James
  Vegetable Universal Pill 73
Mormons 98
Morning Chronicle 54
Morning Post 79

Morrison, Susan vi, vii, viii
Morton, Howard iii. *See* Macfarlane, Helen

Natal xxx
Natal Emigration and Colonization Company xxix
National Charter Association. *See* Chartism
National Parliamentary and Financial Reform Association 24, 28, 41, 44, 52, 60, 69
Neale, E. Vansittart 55
New Poor Law 2
Newtown 65
Norman Conquest 31–32
Northern Star x, xxix, 25
novel ii

O'Connor, Feargus x, 23, 25
  'Land Plan' xxix
O'Hara, Kane 91
old mole 37
Owen, Robert 42, 44, 68

Paine, Thomas
  Rights of Man 57, 66
Palmerston, Lord 52
pantheism iv, xi–xiv, 6–22, 107–110
Parliamentary Reform Bill (1832) 21, 24, 34, 41, 49, 69, 87
Parmenides xv
Peel, Sir Robert 59–64, 63
Penny Magazine 54
Peter the Hermit 3
Philippe, Louis ix, 4, 20, 46
philosophy 9
Pinkard, Terry i
Pitt, William 81
Plato 12–13
The Poor Man's Guardian 2
Pope Pius IX 103
Priestley, Joseph 81
Prior, Matthew 49
prostitution. *See* women: prostitution
Protestantism 7, 38, 103, 107–109
Proust, Consuela Pauline Roland xxix
  dies xxx
Proust, Francis xxix–xxx

Reden, Friedrich Wilhelm von 73
Red Republican iii, x, 55, 57
  threatened with closure 57
Reformation xxiii, 5, 7, 30, 107, 108
Revolutions of 1848 xxvi–xxvii
  Austria-Hungary ix, 4, 80
  France ix, 4
  Germany 1, 87
  Italy 52, 80
  Poland xxviii
Richard II 33
robbery 18
Robespierre, Maximilian 57, 66
Robinson Crusoes 47
Roland, Pauline xxix
Roman Catholicism 16, 89, 103–110
Rome / Roman Empire 12–14, 21, 34, 84, 120
Rothschild, Sir Anthony Nathan de 80
rotten boroughs 41
Rousseau, Jean-Jacques 57
Ruge, Arnold xxvii
Russell, Lord John 39, 40, 43, 45, 63, 104–110
Russia 3, 48, 52

Saint-Simon, Henri de 45
Sands, George xxix
Schapper, Karl xxvi–xxvii, xxviii
Schelling, Friedrich Wilhelm xiv
Schoyen, Albert Robert x
sects 16, 109
Shakespeare xxiv, 21
  A Midsummer Night's Dream 55
  Hamlet 107
  Macbeth 12
  The Merchant of Venice 53, 81
  The Tempest 47
Sharpe, Alexander 104
Shelley, Percy Bysshe ii
skilly 20
slavery. *See* America: slavery
Sophocles v, x, 84
Sparta 77
Spenser, Shelagh xxix
Spinoza, Baruch xi, xiii
  substance xiv–xv

St Ambrose 17
Stamp Duty 2, 19, 57
St Athanasius 99
St Augustine 18
St Basil 18
Stenhouse, Helen (mother) vii
  radical family vii–viii
Stevenson, Gerda vi, viii
St Gregory the Great 17
Stock Exchange 31, 55
St Paul
  "he that will not work, neither shall he eat" 56, 57, 88
Strauss, David xix
  The Life of Jesus Critically Examined ii, xvi–xviii, xxii, 55
Studio Ghibli xxvi

Ten Hours Act 27, 41, 95
Third Estate 32
Thirty-nine Articles 38, 105, 106
Thompson, Edward Palmer
  The Making of the English Working Class xxiv
transcendental ego xiv
'Turkey Red' bandanas vii

United States 48
universal suffrage 52, 62, 94, 109

Vienna ix, 4, 72, 87
Villars, Claude de 23

Walmsley, Sir Joshua 26, 41, 50, 52, 59, 69
Walpole, Horace
  on Mary Wollstonecraft iii
Whig Theory of History 29
Wilberforce, WIlliam 60
William of Orange 30
Williams, Joseph 104
William the Conqueror 31
Willich, August xxviii
Wiseman, Cardinal Nicholas 103
Wollstonecraft, Mary
  "a hyena in petticoats" iii
women
  and children 15, 41, 49, 53–54, 72
  oppression iii, 2, 19, 41, 48, 49, 110

prostitution 15, 49, 54, 64, 95
rape 9
workers 41, 54, 85
Working Mans Advocate 97
World League of Revolutionary Socialists xxvi–xxvii
Wyclif, John 7

Yang, Manuel xxiv
Yeoman, Louise vi, vii, viii, xxiii, xxix
Yoshimoto, Taka'aki xxiv
Young England Party 33

Zoroaster 22

Unkant Books

Splitting in Two: Mad Pride and Punk Rock Oblivion
Robert Dellar
ISBN: 978-0-9926509-0-2
Published: Mar 2014, 232pp

Robert Dellar's reminiscences impart a strange, unwholesome joy, like smoking a cig dipped in popper juice. The only response to the atrocious farce of modern life has to be this savage laughter.
Out to Lunch

In this incendiary slice of under-the-radar British social history we meet everyone from Ronnie Corbett to a Broadmoor inmate whose index offence was the subject of a D-Notice. Robert Dellar's anti-authoritarian and take-no-prisoners spirit of mischief makes it possible for readers of every persuasion to find something to offend their sensibilities.
Simon Morris (Ceramic Hobs)

Derelicts: Thought Worms From the Wreckage
Esther Leslie
ISBN: 978-0-9568176-9-3
Published: Mar 2014, 254pp

Philosophy and art with the imagination to actually change the world: this is the unfinished dream of history and the heart of the revolutionary modernism of the early 20th century, which globalised war and exploitation managed indefinitely to defer. Esther Leslie reopens the cold case on filmmakers, artists, thinkers and other animals, exiled or otherwise Disneyfied, and finds still-warm fertile ground for a wild future as yet unfulfilled. From ideal homes with traces erased to utopian rivers drawn back to their source, the alienated subject of history discerns its rightful place in the present tense, with no room for buts or half-measures. The derelicts of history find new life beyond commodified thought: would that the same could be said for all their readers.
Michael Tencer

Unkant Books

Cosmic Orgasm: The Music of Iancu Dumitrescu
Andy Wilson (ed)
ISBN: 978-0-9568176-5-5
Published: May 2013, 406pp

As a creator of radical music that breaks convention, riding on the edge of the classical avant garde onto realms more closely associated with the likes of Nurse With Wound or The Hafler Trio, Iancu Dumitrescu has the talent to lure you in, mystify and startle with unnerving ferocity.

Alan Freeman

Of all living composers, Dumitrescu is the one who has most exploded sound. Dumitrescu's work is a negation, from the depths, of everything in contemporary music symptomatic of distraction, of banalisation, and of a radical loss of purpose. His music is not a new convolution in the knot of modern music, but an unravelling of the curse.

Tim Hodgkinson

Azmud
Ken Fox
ISBN: 978-0-9568176-4-8
Published: Mar 2013, 270pp

Drifting in and out of sense as in an interrupted dream, Azmud is a novel contribution to literary art as political allegory. In each of its five sections—'expired generations'—it attempts to retell the tale of the human psyche, the damage it has undergone under capitalism, in the form of a wandering work tribe searching for value in the spectacular flow of mass communication, on behalf of various severe 'generals' who demand a quota of abstract accumulation. But each of Azmud's industrial adventures in turn become allegories for the act of the text's own creation. But what happens in Azmud? Under orders, a human herd wanders thru the dense miasma of mass communication, hunting for precious ox-ore to stash in their air-ark or fuel their ancient steam engine. A vagrant crew invades the broken dreams of a drowsy industrial tycoon, stealing baskets full of his precious sleep. A homeless hoard combs thru post-industrial litter, searching for burnable rubble. A fake engineer captures a team of lost work-horses and four mammoth protozoans to help boost the energy yield of his toxic currents. A cargo ship collects a crew of stranded industrial outcasts with their precious ark full of ore and its tyrannical captain subjects them to relentless injections and many unwanted adventures.

Association of Musical Marxists

Unkant Books

More Years for the Locust
Jim Higgins
ISBN: 978-0-9568176-3-1
Published: Jun 2012, 330pp

There is a human scale to the story so often missing in the more staid accounts of the left and its history which often create an artificial barrier between readers and the activists being written about, who were after all, people much like them. This dimension of the book which, to put it bluntly, makes it such a good laugh, also provides a great store of what Aristotle would have called practical wisdom. The laughter and the nous are here very closely related and impossible to summarise, they must be read...

The trouble with Higgins is ultimately our own trouble. The reward for recognising this is to be able to rehabilitate and nourish a part of ourselves. The IS tradition is broader than the latest line or missive from the latest CC. This may seem a problem to some but it ought to be seen as a great resource. Revolutionaries too have traditions. Perhaps we are now in a position to learn from Higgins even if we were sadly a bit too stupid to do so before.

John Game

Blake in Cambridge
Ben Watson
ISBN: 978-0-9568176-8-6
Published: Apr 2012, 168pp

Blake in Cambridge was written after reading William Blake's visionary epic Milton during extended bouts of childcare in Coram's Fields in the summer of 2010. Blake in Cambridge is the Marxist critique of Eng. Lit. Christopher Caudwell was meant to write, but screwed up due to a CPGB sociology which denies literature the chance to answer back. In Marx's polemic, the jokes of Tristram Shandy and Don Quixote became weapons in class struggle. This, argues Watson, is how Blake can and should be used.

Unkant Books
1839: The Chartist Insurrection
David Black and Chris Ford
ISBN: 978-0-9568176-6-2
Published: Apr 2012, 268pp

With its meticulous attention to detailed sources, its comprehensive scope and its exacting research, this book doesn't just address the neglect of this important and interesting episode in Labour movement history, but more importantly it also challenges us to think again about the revolutionary potential of the British Labour movement.

John McDonnell MP, *Foreword*

The Struggle for Hearts and Minds: Essays on the Second World War
Ray Challinor
ISBN: 978-0-9568176-1-7
Published: Sep 2011, 128pp

This book of essays is a shocking read, but the shocks arrive from the history itself, not sensationalist writing. We've been told that the Second World War was a war against evil waged by the goodhearted and true. The spectre of Hitler and Nazism is invoked every time NATO bombs are aimed at a defenceless country.

In his scathing account of ruling-class fears, plans and allegiances, Ray Challinor shows how much their every move was governed by competition and self-interest—and anxieties about popular reaction. His evidence shatters the comforting national myth which has been spun around the cataclysm—and shows that people, working-class people, do not like killing each other, they had to be cajoled and manipulated into doing so.

Unkant

Read Ray Challinor's, The Struggle for Hearts and Minds, *to learn the truth, not just about the Second World War, but of the eternal truth about war: They were bombing Iraqi villages in 1923.*

Sharon Borthwick, *Unkant*

Unkant Books

Happiness: Poems After Rimbaud
Sean Bonney
ISBN: 978-0-9568176-6-2
Published: Sep 2011, 128pp

It is impossible to fully grasp Rimbaud's work, and especially Une Saison en Enfer, if you have not studied through and understood the whole of Marx's Capital. And this is why no English speaking poet has ever understood Rimbaud. Poetry is stupid, but then again, stupidity is not the absence of intellectual ability but rather the scar of its mutilation.

Rimbaud hammered out his poetic programme in 1871, just as the Paris Commune was being blown off the map. He wanted to be there. It's all he talked about. The "systematic derangement of the senses" is the social senses, ok, and the "I" becomes an "other" as in the transformation of the individual into the collective when it all kicks off. It's only in the English speaking world you have to point simple shit like that out. But then again, these poems have **NOTHING TO DO WITH RIMBAUD.** *If you think they're translations you're an idiot. In the enemy language it is necessary to lie.*

Adorno for Revolutionaries
Ben Watson
ISBN: 978-0-9568176-0-0
Published: May 2011, 256pp

Starting with the commodity form (rather than the 'spirit' lauded by everyone from Classic FM retards to NME journalists), Adorno outlined a revolutionary musicology, a passageway between subjective feeling and objective conditions. In Adorno for Revolutionaries, Ben Watson argues that this is what everyone's been looking for since the PCF blackened the name of Marxism by wrecking the hopes of May '68. Batting aside postmodern prattlers and candyass pundits alike, this collection detonates the explosive core of Adorno's thought. Those 'socialists' who are frightened of their feelings can go stew in their imaginary bookshop. For us, great music is a necessity. To talk about it is to criticise everything that exists.

Association of Musical Marxists

For those who have the ears to hear I strongly recommend Adorno For Revolutionaries as a substantial and very readable effort.

David Black, *Hobgoblin*

Lightning Source UK Ltd.
Milton Keynes UK
UKHW011344271220
375899UK00003B/540

9 780992 650919